AA004077

ICONS 2023

The Eighteenth International Conference on Systems

April 24th – 28th, 2023

Venice, Italy

ICONS 2023 Editors

Oliver Michler, Technical University Dresden, Germany

Printed from e-media with permission by:

Curran Associates, Inc.
57 Morehouse Lane
Red Hook, NY 12571

Some format issues inherent in the e-media version may also appear in this print version.

International Academy, Research, and Industry Association (IARIA)
412 Derby Way
Wilmington, DE 19810

Phone: (408) 893-6407
Fax: (408) 527-6351

petre@iaria.org

Additional copies of this publication are available from:

Curran Associates, Inc.
57 Morehouse Lane
Red Hook, NY 12571 USA
Phone: 845-758-0400
Fax: 845-758-2633
Email: curran@proceedings.com
Web: www.proceedings.com

Table of Contents

ICONS 2023

Forward

The Eighteenth International Conference on Systems (ICONS 2023), held between April 24th and April 28th, 2023, continued a series of events covering fundamentals on designing, implementing, testing, validating, and maintaining various kinds of software and hardware systems. The topics were addresses from theory to practice, in terms of methodologies, design, implementation, testing, use cases, tools, and lessons learnt.

In the last years, new system concepts have been promoted and partially embedded in new deployments. Anticipative systems, autonomic and autonomous systems, self-adapting systems, or on-demand systems are systems exposing advanced features. These features demand special requirements specification mechanisms, advanced behavioral design patterns, special interaction protocols, and flexible implementation platforms. Additionally, they require new monitoring and management paradigms, as self-protection, self-diagnosing, self-maintenance become core design features.

The design of application-oriented systems is driven by application-specific requirements that have a very large spectrum. Despite the adoption of uniform frameworks and system design methodologies supported by appropriate models and system specification languages, the deployment of application-oriented systems raises critical problems. Specific requirements in terms of scalability, real-time, security, performance, accuracy, distribution, and user interaction drive the design decisions and implementations.

This leads to the need for gathering application-specific knowledge and develop particular design and implementation skills that can be reused in developing similar systems.

Validation and verification of safety requirements for complex systems containing hardware, software and human subsystems must be considered from early design phases. There is a need for rigorous analysis of the role of people and process causing hazards within safety-related systems; however, these claims are often made without a rigorous analysis of the human factors involved. Accurate identification and implementation of safety requirements for all elements of a system, including people and procedures become crucial in complex and critical systems, especially in safety-related projects from the civil aviation, defense health, and transport sectors.

Fundamentals on safety-related systems concern both positive (desired properties) and negative (undesired properties) aspects. Safety requirements are expressed at the individual equipment level and at the operational-environment level. However, ambiguity in safety requirements may lead to reliable unsafe systems. Additionally, the distribution of safety requirements between people and machines makes difficult automated proofs of system safety. This is somehow obscured by the difficulty of applying formal techniques (usually used for equipment-related safety requirements) to derivation and satisfaction of human-related safety requirements (usually, human factors techniques are used).

We take here the opportunity to warmly thank all the members of the ICONS 2023 technical program committee, as well as all the reviewers. The creation of such a high-quality conference program would not have been possible without their involvement. We also kindly thank all the authors who dedicated much of their time and effort to contribute to ICONS 2023. We truly believe that, thanks to all these efforts, the final conference program consisted of top-quality contributions. We also thank the members of the ICONS 2023 organizing committee for their help in handling the logistics of this event.

We hope that ICONS 2023 was a successful international forum for the exchange of ideas and results between academia and industry and for the promotion of progress in the area of systems.

ICONS 2023 Chairs

ICONS 2023 Steering Committee

ICONS 2023 Publicity Chairs

ICONS 2023
Committee

ICONS 2023 Steering Committee

David Inkermann, Technische Universität Clausthal, Institute of Mechanical Engineering, Germany
Christoph Knieke, Technische Universität Clausthal, Institute for Software and Systems Engineering, Germany
Giulio Telleschi, MBDA, Italy
Mo Mansouri, Stevens Institute of Technology, USA, University of South-Eastern Norway, Norway
Mark Austin, University of Maryland, USA
Gerrit Muller, University of South-Eastern Norway, Norway, TNO - Eindhoven, The Netherlands

ICONS 2023 Publicity Chairs

Laura Garcia, Universitat Politecnica de Valencia, Spain
Javier Rocher Morant, Universitat Politecnica de Valencia, Spain

ICONS 2023 Technical Program Committee

Qammer H. Abbasi, University of Glasgow, Scotland, UK
Mohamed A. Abd El Ghany, German University in Cairo, Egypt
Witold Abramowicz, Poznan University of Economics, Poland
Afaq Ahmad, Sultan Qaboos University, Oman
Abdelouhab Aitouche, YNCREA/HEI | University of Lille, France
Ali Al-Humairi, German University of Technology (GUtech), Oman
Walid Al-Hussaibi, Southern Technical University (STU), Iraq
Mohammed Al-Khafajiy, University of Reading, UK
Saloua Bel Hadj Ali, University of Tunis-El Manar / University of Gabès, Tunisia
Fady Alnajjar, United Arab Emirates University, UAE
Marc Austin, University Of Maryland, USA
Muhammed Ali Aydin, Istanbul University-Cerrahpasa, Turkey
Snježana Babić, Juraj Dobrila University of Pula, Croatia
Lubomir Bakule, Institute of Information Theory and Automation, Czech Republic
Walter Balzano, Università degli Studi di Napoli Federico II, Italy
Kamel Barkaoui, Cedric - Cnam, Paris, France
Janibul Bashir, National Institute of Technology, Srinagar, India
Suvadip Batabyal, BITS Pilani, Hyderabad Campus, India
Abir Ben Ali, National School of Computer Sciences (ENSI), Tunisia
Alejandro J. Bianchi, LIVEWARE S.A. / Universidad Catolica Argentina, Argentina
Francesco Bianconi, Università degli Studi di Perugia, Italy
Razvan Bocu, Transilvania University of Brasov, Romania
Birthe Boehm, Siemens AG, Germany
Sander Bohte, Machine Learning group - CWI, Amsterdam, The Netherlands
Marilisa Botte, Federico II University of Naples, Italy
Rahma Boucetta, University of Sfax, Tunisia
Frédéric Bousefsaf, Université de Lorraine, France

Copyright Information

A Five-Factor Market Approach for Long-Term Product Development: A Result of Systems Thinking

Andy Mattulat Filipovic
Department of Mechanical and Industrial Engineering
Norwegian University of Science and Technology
Trondheim, Norway
email: filipovic.a.mattulat@ntnu.no

Mo Mansouri
Faculty of Technology, Natural Sciences, and Maritime Sciences
University of South-Eastern Norway
Kongsberg, Norway
email: mo.mansouri@usn.no

Abstract— **Current product development practices face challenges when adapting to long-term changes in early-stage development. This challenge happens due to missing awareness of the future dynamic conditions that influence future market conditions. This paper introduces five factors to investigate the future dynamic complexities for product development organizations. Findings show interdependencies between the factors, Business model, Politics and regulation, Trends, Funding and Insurance, and Technology. Each factor consists of an individual system, which can be influenced by each other over time. Further investigation of the interdependencies linking five factors set out to reveal the new and unexplored potential for product development organizations. The paper introduces a systemic approach to facing future challenges of managing long-term product development management.**

Keywords- Systems of systems; Future market.

I. Introduction

Today, we face the challenge of missing the objectives of the Paris agreement if we continue to produce and develop technologies as we have been doing so far [1] [2]. When managing their project portfolios nowadays, companies have already faced the challenge of predicting short-market conditions as the market is rapidly changing.

However, with the increasing complexity of the world and increasing numbers of near-tipping-point incidents over the last year, the war in Europe, the rising cost of goods, etc., is the green transition, something we all need to participate in. Changes will not emerge by themselves and arise in a magical moment but need development through innovation and research.

For decades, scholars and researchers have claimed that modern product development stresses increased demand for new incremental solutions and is more complex than ever. Could it be that no matter when we develop new technologies, we anticipate the current situation full of unrecognized possibilities and risks and, therefore, see it as the challenges of the time? Therefore, by acknowledging the complexity of the socio-technical, environmental complex reality, we need a dynamic framework for dealing with the dynamics in the complexity or reality to distinguish between complex structures and complicated mechanisms.

Systems thinking is known in multiple works of literature for being able to grasp systems complexity, visualize interdependencies, create an understanding of boundaries, and many more valuable things. Therefore, this makes systems thinking suitable for addressing systems complexity, as we do in this article.

The future market will remain dynamic, and nothing will appear in 10 years as it does today. Moreover, as we acknowledge that market conditions are rapidly changing, we need a framework to identify future uncertainties to help guide organizational development.

The research goal of this paper is to explore the holistic landscape, from an enterprise perspective, for interrelated systems of systems that together shape the conditions for the future development of products and systems. This sum of information from the five factors introduced in this paper, can support portfolio managers in design- and decision-making processes to allocate resources best towards the organizations long-term strategy.

The structure of the paper consists of six sections, where Section I continues to introduce a background overview of and establishes the challenges the paper addresses. Section II presents the methods used in producing the results. Section III introduces the five factors of the market. Section IV addresses some of the direct dynamics in the system. Section V places the five factors into the system of product development introduced in Section I. Section VI concludes and addresses further research.

A. *Background*

Product development of physical products is becoming more complex as requirements for the green transition are adopted. The green transition influences all product life cycle stages, including the whole value chain [3].

While many companies have adopted some form of an agile workflow in areas of organizations, the portfolio management processes often follow a waterfall–stage gate approach for governing the whole enterprise [4]. This approach has some shortcomings in the later stages of development, where the data collected as part of testing is not returned into the process to feed the early innovation activities (see Figure 1).

Figure 1 illustrates the current portfolio practice in a typical stage gate approach. The flow of the main activities follows from the left top to the bottom right side. At the top, project sponsors provide input on requirements, evaluate the project, and approve the project to continue to the following

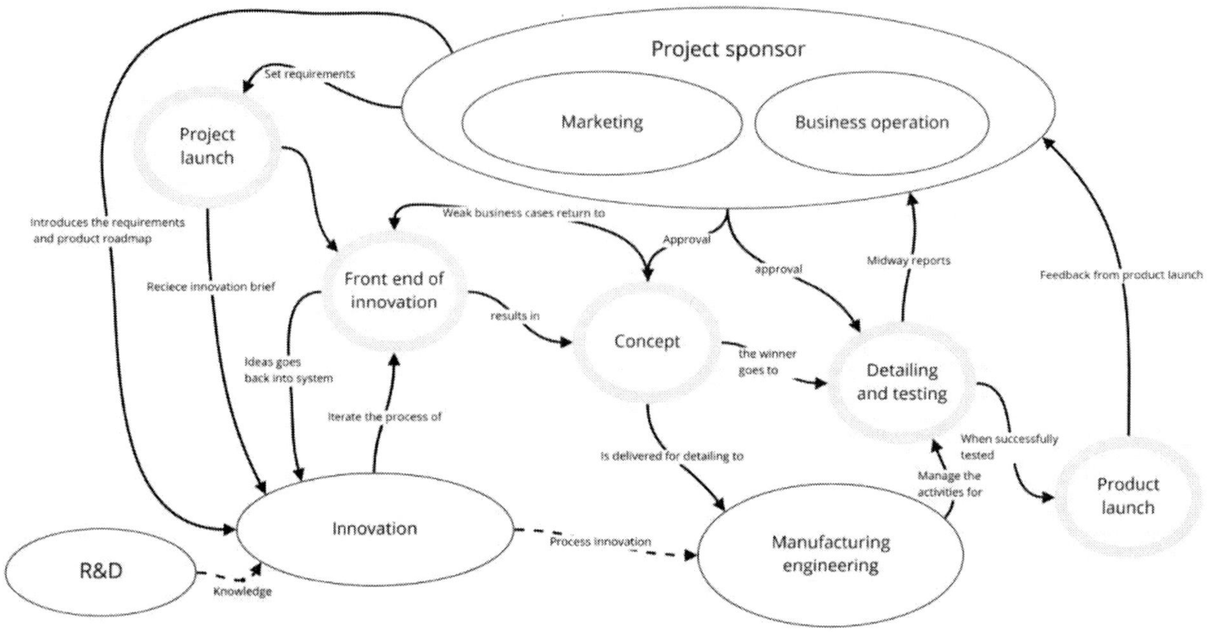

Figure 1. Innovation system of systems.

stages of development. Innovation consists of activities involving inputs from research and development and detailed information on innovation projects and requirements. The output for the process can be in concept ideas or process innovation to improve areas like manufacturing. Manufacturing is responsible for evaluating the concept requirements and manufacturing processes align and make it possible to deliver products that fulfill requirements in cost and quality.

Existing product development practices get the specifications and requirements from various sources (for example, customer interviews, product testing, and sales numbers) [5]. The current way may be holistic but ignores the dynamic perspective of potential future requirements.

Other researchers have addressed uncertainty in project portfolio management and product development of radical innovation [6] [7]. Despite recognizing certain interdependencies, this area has not yet been properly investigated, particularly when it comes to long-term uncertainties in dynamic systems. The traditional product development and innovation methodologies treat each system as singular units, such as law and regulation or technology, and so forth. Thereby overlooking how these seemingly independent systems influence one another by, for example, how technology helps shape and form new laws and regulations by setting collecting data for science-based targets and, consequently, miss addressing the circumstances that enable this dynamic. By ignoring the whole picture, we believe that opportunities and potential are overlooked for systems innovations that truly can impact society and the environment.

B. Challenge

The challenge in the existing systems is the missing consideration of long-term conditions related to each aspect of the system. Various uncertainties must be managed throughout development as potential risks are involved in new product development.

Traditional product development practices tend to look at various inputs to the product development process, taking "influencing factors" as a static parameter in the design process. However, the different factors of uncertainty in product development practices are not static and independent. The individual requirements are, over time, dynamic and connected through mechanisms and processes.

The existing approach for evaluating the influencing factors in product development and portfolio management is segmented and shared between operational units in the organization. The challenge, in this case, as time is a factor, is that implications made in one area of the system will not immediately result in changed behavior in all other affected system elements.

The finite purpose of an organization is to provide products or services to bring value to a market in exchange for money. As the market will be dynamic over time, we see the market as constructed from different influencing factors. Therefore, we will spend the rest of this paper constructing a systems framework to consider the influencing factors that shape the future context for the enterprise and introduce those into the earlier described product development practice. We do this to raises awareness of the interdependencies within the context where organizations develop and deliver products and services. Exploration of uncertainties is essential for designers and managers within product development. Hence, they can focus their innovation and possibilities on managing development and resources by understanding each element and its dynamics within their working systems and how these address the circumstances and requirements that affect their projects.

II. METHOD

The data for the system identification was discovered and structured using Checkland's Soft system model [5] [6]. The model introduces a 7-step process where steps 1-4 consist of identifying the existing system and developing a conceptual model of the system in an iterative process. Step 5 uses the conceptual model and learning to raise discussion of challenges in the existing system, which are desirable and feasible. Step 6 consists of developing a suggested to-be version acceptable for all the including world views. Step 7 is to implement the suggested changes into the analyzed system. This final step is out of the scope of this article.

During identifying the different subsystem agents, relations, interfaces, and boundaries, we used the acronym CATWOE to identify the reactive forces and their roots [10]. CATWOE stands for, Customers – identifies who gains or losses value in the process, Actors – identifies who implements the active element, Transformation – What the functions in the system transform, World view – Justification of the system's existence, Owner – Who can establish changes to the system, and Environment – the external condition and constraints.

Finally, a systemigram is a method to introduce the system story of how future strategic impact might benefit companies in their product development [11].

III. INTRODUCTION TO THE SYSTEM

We see the high-level system of systems consisting of five subsystems each as a market influencing factors. Each contributes to shaping the market conditions where the organization operates. Figure 2 shows the five subsystems named: Business model, Technology, Political and regulatory, Trends, and Funding and insurance. The dynamics in the system of systems are complex due to the high number of agents involved in the activities related to each subsystem. Therefore, each following introduction of the subsystems happens in isolation. It is worth noting that, in Figure 2, no human actors are included, but all mentioned elements only exist due to the development and influence of groups and individuals.

A. *Business model*

The business model is at the core of the system activity, and it is expected of the organization to know its capabilities, placement in the market, and product assortment [12]. The purpose of placing the business model as the core activity is that the company fully controls this element and can adjust accordingly to changes in other systems. Furthermore, a resilient business model can adapt to changes in the remainder of the system.

B. *Technological field*

The technological fields include existing internal technologies. Technology covers projects in all stages of development, from the conceptual ideas to the preparation for product launch as well as experimental technologies under research and development, existing patents, competing technologies, and planned concepts that already exist in the technological pipeline or road maps.

External technologies are also included and can consist of existing competitive technologies and technologies under development in other companies.

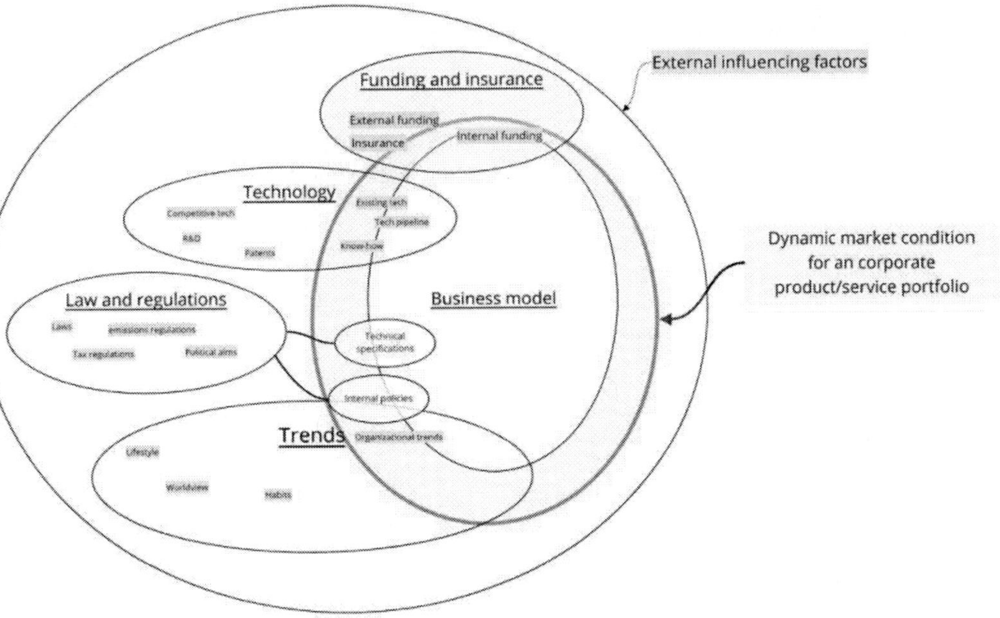

Figure 2. Market influencing systems of systems.

C. *The political and regulatory system*

The political and regulatory system consists of sections and units working with and developing standards, laws, and regulations. The purpose of this system is to convert political decisions into tools when implemented, either reinforcing a specific systemic behavior or diminishing a systemic behavior. For example, the political decision in the EU parliament to ban throwaway plastic has led to an expansion in the market of single-use cutlery made of wood and bamboo [13].

D. *Trends*

Specific trends release opportunities for technology development. Therefore, trends are a vital part, of the dynamics, of shaping the existing and future markets. We identify elements in the Trend systems, including lifestyle trends, for example, equality, work-life balance, and Eco-friendly. Other trends including working trends. An example where we have seen movement, especially during the Corona virus pandemic, was when the work environment accepted remote workdays. Such changes open new opportunities for technologies to emerge. Furthermore, we also see organizational trends, which are trends within the management of organizations. For example, new work methods influence the working environment and work behavior.

E. *Finance and insurance*

Innovation of technologies is highly dependent on the sources of finance supporting development and research. Funding sources can come from internal sources in the organization's budget or external funding by various public and private funds or governmental support.

Some studies indicate high support from governmental funds to support technological development to push society in the desired direction [14]. This is placing financial risk in institutions and constellations where profit is not the overarching purpose. As a result, funding is addressing research activities and specific technological flagship projects that might create a leap in technological development.

Inventing and developing new technologies involves high risks as many uncertainties are related to new and untested technologies. Therefore, insurance of the development activities during the process is essential. Furthermore, insurance of the testing facilities and human interaction is essential and impacts the decisions of what technologies are tested and at what speed technologies can be carried forward.

F. *Outside of the system*

Outside of the drawn system of systems, we have the macro environment. The model does not include the macro environment because of its reduced effect on the direct subsystems identified earlier. Elements such as resources and materials would be relevant to discuss but are left out of the system mapping since resources and materials are subcomponents for multiple subsystems described earlier. Materials are expected to be a limited resource based on laws and regulations. Also, the tendencies of what the products will consist of are highly dependent on the technology and requirements of the product. Requirements towards material and resources need to follow the regulations of, for example, production, consumption, and recyclability, to name a few. Finally, when discussing materials and resources, companies conduct a cost-benefit analysis of optimizing the specific products for the conditions they will meet in their life cycle. This optimization also relates to insurance as the selection of materials relates to the requirements of robustness needed for the specific technology or product. These different factors are analyzed together with the company's business model.

Other researchers might argue that the market condition is a vital factor for the future approach. We have decided not to include market dynamics because the interdependencies between multiple factors will cover market behavior. For example, political implications can assign regulations in the form of taxation or subsidies that can adjust sales mechanisms and regulate the market of products and services. Such regulations can be combined with production mechanisms used to produce goods or services.

From an enterprise perspective, the business model influences the shaping of market trends. Does the company decide for a fixed production output, or is production possible to adjust? What are the customer relations, and how do the additional factors impact the supply chain?

Trends consists of direction and dynamic patterns within each systems of finance, politics, technology, and human behavior. Trends will, therefore, influence the possibilities and behavior of the market. The result is when reviewing the factors as a function of time, the five factors are all involved as shaping forces for the future market where each factor contributes, individually and as part of a whole, to the behavior of the future market and its dynamics.

IV. THE DYNAMIC IN THE SYSTEM AND HOW THE SYSTEMS REACTS TO CHANGES

Undoubtedly, when looking at the isolated system's elements, it is, in the short term, easy to say that each system is quite static. However, when investigating the influencing factors on the market over an extended period, it becomes apparent that shaping forces influence each other.

Technology development happens according to the company's business model and strategy. Technology development is largely related to the available financial resources, is influenced by the political landscape, and gets constrained by regulations and restrictions in the technological area. The technology takes its form from existing trends in the technology environment, developed through further specifications and requirements, both technical and non-technical. The existing reality also shows how new emerging technologies help shape the political landscape, which becomes evident if we consider what has happened within cyber security, education, and healthcare over the last century. Furthermore, when planned and distributed in certain ways, technologies can support the creation of new trends within society, considering what Apple has done. New technologies such as artificial intelligence also help the Funding and insurance market take risk assessments, decide where to invest, and provide investments and security. Finally, technology is also the source for establishing new business models within organizations and companies.

Politics and regulation are one source of new emerging technologies. Funding in development and limitations in legal targets for emission force companies to develop new business models. The political agenda and regulations can also set forward new market trends or trends in public.

The company can also develop a new **business model** that inspires innovative technological development. A part of the business model could also be to investigate how to collect the right among the right source of funding to execute experimental development. Another business model interaction can focus on where politics and regulation might be obsolete within a particular technological field. The value behind such activity could aim at being the first mover and the first to exploit a new market condition. Being the first to get a license to produce or reuse a specific resource could lead to profit and gain the most significant market shares.

Funding and insurance is a vital shaping force in the future market. Particular funding opens up new opportunities for companies to test concepts and ideas, lowering the individual risk of the company going bankrupt or out of business. Companies must still consider insurance as a vital part of new product development. If the company develops a "new to the world technology," it is vital for the people involved, the environment, and the company itself to have security in place. The company's guidelines might support the development of a safe environment until it can be approved as a potential as a future technology.

Trend will also shape future market conditions based on public trends, but trends within technology path dependencies might be challenging to break. If public trans goes into grass root movements, there is a possibility for a new emerging company providing new unseen technical solutions to the marketplace. However, it could also impact the political and regulatory system, especially since grassroots movements tend to collect inspiring people with much energy to push the system into creating their agenda. Due to the private trends, companies must adapt their business models to meet social trends and public awareness. Furthermore, in funding and insurance, there will probably be certain trends within specific areas, for example, green investments portfolios in pension funds, but these trends also shape the public perception of the company's reputation

V. The Suggested New System

Figure 3 shows a systemigram of how the new optimized system brings knowledge of the new market condition into the development complexity. We find it helpful to place the five-factor system at the front end of innovation, where market tendencies are researched and explored. The system of a new future market condition should feed the innovation process and inspire new ideas based on potential opportunities in future markets. In addition, the system analysis can feed the top management with information from scenario creation, with uncertainties and potential risks to consider in planning the company's future. Based on the explorative knowledge, the top management gets a better source of information on to base their prediction and decisions. Even though this process does not eliminate the uncertainty, it visualizes and brings forward the uncertainties of the future, and by visualizing future challenges, it allows the company to react and make decisions on how to deal with the uncertainties. Top management can decide to investigate uncertainties and quantify them as risks or opportunities. This investigation will undoubtedly spark inspiration toward innovation projects and new areas to

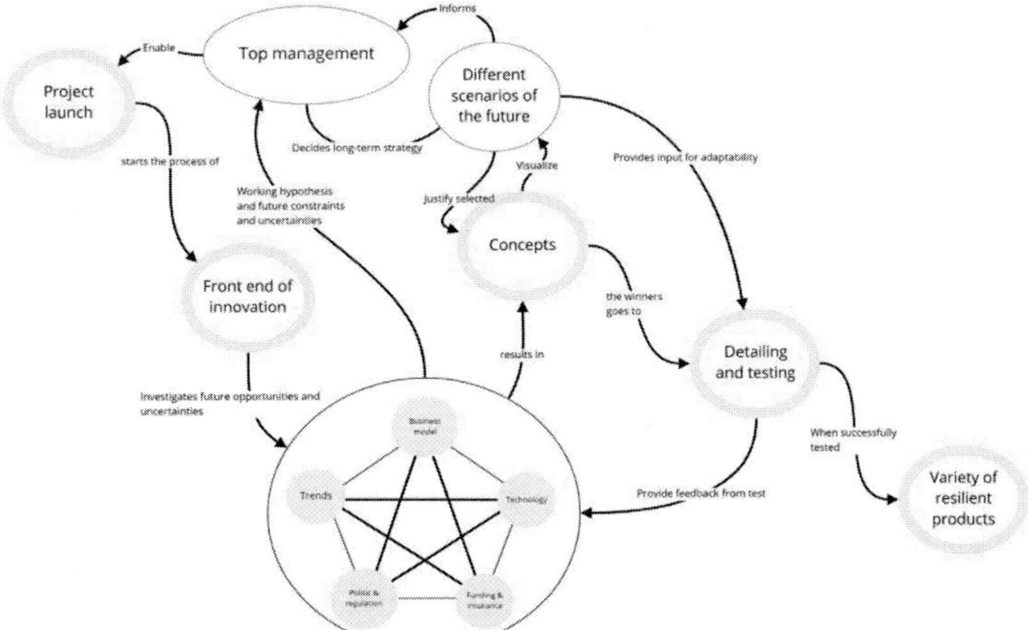

Figure 3. System suggestion for improved market exploration

investigate in the future. As in the old system, top management will evaluate conceptual ideas, but now there is an integrated feedback loop that feeds the latest market-testing and prototype-testing market conditions into the innovation process. The innovation process will catch any change or realization in the testing phase and work as input and constraints in the next iteration. Finally, uncertainties and risks identified in the future scenarios can be included in the product development process to be strengthened and prepared in the pipeline for the next module; this leads to more resilient/adaptable/flexible solutions or technologies to meet future conditions.

VI. CONCLUSION

The research goal set in this paper is to examine the holistic landscape of market-related systems that shape future conditions of products and systems and how information can feed portfolio design- and decision-making.

Through a systems perspective of the organization interfaces with market conditions, and acknowledgment of the future market as dynamic, this paper identifies five factors: Business model, Technology, Political and regulatory, Trends, and Funding and insurance. The paper discusses how these factors are systems of systems and are interrelated and, through various relations, shape the conditions around future solutions. These relations are highly context depended, and every change to a system will influence the possibilities within the system.

Therefore, we suggest using the factors as interrelated systems to analyze future market conditions. We found the system valuable in the front end of innovation within the innovation portfolio exploration and development process. Here, it informs the organization's innovation team and top management with helpful identification of future scenarios and addresses interrelations that might hold business potential that demands further investigation and innovation resources.

Further studies from this field will be industry-related case studies to map the interrelation and identify the relations and actors that shape the dynamics. Furthermore, an analysis of how the interdependencies influence portfolio managers' decision-making. Finally, we will address what to consider what to consider when reviewing the system and analyzing future conditions when establishing and aligning requirements to address and solve societal- and environmental challenges?

REFERENCES

[1] D. M. Smith *et al.*, "Predicted Chance That Global Warming Will Temporarily Exceed 1.5 °C," *Geophys. Res. Lett.*, vol. 45, no. 21, pp. 11,895-11,903, Nov. 2018, doi: 10.1029/2018GL079362.

[2] R. P. Barston, "The Paris agreement," in *Modern Diplomacy*, 2019, pp. 492–505. doi: 10.4324/9781351270090-20.

[3] WBCSD and WRI, "Corporate Value Chain (Scope 3) Accounting and Reporting Standard – Supplement to the GHG Protocol Corporate Accounting and Reporting Standard," *Greenhouse Gas Protocol*. 2011.

[4] R. G. Cooper and A. F. Sommer, "New-Product Portfolio Management with Agile," *Res. Manag.*, vol. 63, no. 1, pp. 29–38, Jan. 2020, doi: 10.1080/08956308.2020.1686291.

[5] R. Cooper, A. Wootton, and M. Bruce, "Requirements capture as process of technology-market integration," *Int. J. Technol. Manag.*, vol. 17, no. 6, pp. 582–596, 1999, doi: 10.1504/IJTM.1999.002737.

[6] M. Martinsuo, T. Korhonen, and T. Laine, "Identifying, framing and managing uncertainties in project portfolios," *Int. J. Proj. Manag.*, vol. 32, no. 5, pp. 732–746, 2014, doi: 10.1016/j.ijproman.2014.01.014.

[7] G. C. O'Connor and M. P. Rice, "A Comprehensive Model of Uncertainty Associated with Radical Innovation," *J. Prod. Innov. Manag.*, vol. 30, no. SUPPL 1, pp. 2–18, Dec. 2013, doi: 10.1111/jpim.12060.

[8] P. Checkland and J. Poulter, "Soft Systems Methodology," in *Systems Approaches to Making Change: A Practical Guide*, Springer, London, 2020, pp. 201–253. doi: 10.1007/978-1-4471-7472-1_5.

[9] P. Checkland, "Soft systems methodology: A thirty year retrospective," *Syst. Res. Behav. Sci.*, vol. 17, no. SUPPL., pp. 11–58, 2000, doi: 10.1002/1099-1743(200011)17:1+<::aid-sres374>3.0.co;2-o.

[10] B. Bergvall-Kåreborn, A. Mirijamdotter, and A. Basden, "Basic principles of SSM modeling: An examination of CATWOE from a soft perspective," *Systemic Practice and Action Research*, vol. 17, no. 2. pp. 55–73, 2004. doi: 10.1023/B:SPAA.0000018903.18767.18.

[11] L. B. Rainey and A. Tolk, *Modeling and Simulation Support for System of Systems Engineering Applications*. 2015. doi: 10.1002/9781118501757.

[12] D. J. Teece, "Business Models, Business Strategy and Innovation," *Long Range Plann.*, vol. 43, pp. 172–194, doi: 10.1016/j.lrp.2009.07.003.

[13] European Parliament, "Parliament seals ban on throwaway plastics by 2021 | News | European Parliament," *Eur. Parliam.*, pp. 2019–2022, 2019, Accessed: Mar. 21, 2023. [Online]. Available: https://www.europarl.europa.eu/news/en/press-room/20190321IPR32111/parliament-seals-ban-on-throwaway-plastics-by-2021

[14] M. Mazzucato, *The entrepreneurial state : debunking public vs. private sector myths*. S.l.: Penguin, 2018.

A Systems Approach to E-Government Cloud Sustainability

Geoffrey Lichtenheim
School of Systems & Enterprises
Stevens Institute of Technology
Hoboken, USA
email:glichten@stevens.edu

Mo Mansouri
School of Systems & Enterprises
Stevens Institute of Technology
Hoboken, USA
email:mmansour@stevens.edu

Roshanak Nilchiani
School of Systems & Enterprises
Stevens Institute of Technology
Hoboken, USA
email:rnilchia@stevens.edu

Abstract—**The purpose of this study is to explore the use of public cloud computing by the US Federal Government leveraging dynamic systems modeling and system thinking methods. A historical analysis of public cloud hyperscale service provider growth and Federal Government cloud consumption is conducted as a baseline to highlight significant milestones over the past fifteen years. A stakeholder interest map is established to determine the endogenous and exogenous elements of our study, and a novel dynamic model is developed to capture the feedback loops, stocks, and flows, as well as multi-dimensional relationships between the variables presented. To prevent large and potentially harmful oscillations, cloud diversity principles such as interoperability and security are presented which promote both balance and sustainability in the system. The primary hypothesis is that self-reinforcing feedback loops which represent the consumption of public cloud services will be constrained by goal-seeking loops which represent Federal Information Technology (IT) budget limitations and macroeconomic fluctuations. To conclude, areas such as model enhancement through greater quantitative analysis as well as recommendations for further research on this topic are proposed.**

Keywords-E-Government; E-Governance; Public Cloud; System Dynamics; Systems Thinking.

I. Introduction

The US federal IT budget for the fiscal year 2022 is approximately 92.4 billion dollars [1]. Over ten percent of that amount is projected to be utilized towards the consumption of public cloud services by government agencies. This double-digit percentage has increased exponentially over the past five years and appears to accelerate as new use cases are discovered and demand increases. The shift from privately run government data centers to cloud-hosted infrastructure has accelerated over the past decade as security and resiliency of these platforms and services have finally met stringent government compliance requirements [2][3]. With digital transformation initiatives now in progress from multiple areas of government, a new problem is forming and related to increasing spend on these premium cloud services.

With a seemingly endless supply of computing resources available public cloud vendors such as Amazon, Microsoft, and Google have capitalized on the shift from on-premises maintained compute, network, and storage systems to offsite third-party operated platforms. With business agility comes some trade-offs, primarily associated with less control and visibility around the complete spend of managing and maintaining these environments. Cloud vendors are intent on increasing Annual Recurring Revenue (ARR), boosting their share price and overall profitability. While this incentive leads sales teams to position large transformational deals, the customer (in our case, the federal government) must make careful selections and ensure the proper controls are in place to prevent sprawl in the resources provided [4][5][6][7].

In a previously published research paper titled "Preventing E-Government Tragedy Of The Clouds Using System Thinking Methods", we developed a cloud service ontology, used a systemigram to highlight system connections, and proposed a novel cloud efficiency model [8]. In this study, we focus on the multi-dimensional nature of an E-government system leveraging public cloud infrastructure to define causal relationships to understand multi-loop behavior. In Section 2a, a timeline is developed to highlight significant milestones in both E-government use of the public cloud and the beginnings and dynamic growth of the big three hyperscalers, Amazon Web Services, Microsoft Azure, and Google Cloud Platform. In Section 2b, we explore our system's endogenous and exogenous agents with a stakeholder interest map. Section 2c presents a causal loop diagram to display the variables in our system and show the relationship, polarity, and behavior of this multi-loop structure. Section 2d introduces cloud diversity principles, a road map for E-government entities to leverage public cloud resources more efficiently and effectively. We touch upon portability, security, and interoperability of the system to ensure we are creating a future state architecture that is sustainable and resilient. In Section 3, we conclude with our hypothesis, constraints, and ideas for further research to enhance the body of knowledge around this topic.

A. *Definitions*

E-government is defined as the delivery of government services via information and communication technology (ICT) efficiently to both businesses and citizens [9][10]. E-Government refers to the delivery of government services via Information and Communication Technology (ICT) efficiently to Citizens (G2C), Businesses (G2B), Government Employees (G2E), and other Government Entities (G2G). It also infers the use of digital technologies such as computer systems and mobile platforms. Cloud computing, as defined by the National Institute of Standards and Technology (NIST), is "a model for enabling ubiquitous, convenient, on-demand network access to a shared pool of configurable computing resources (e.g., networks, servers, storage, applications, and services) that can be rapidly provisioned and released with minimal management effort or service provider interaction"[1]. Hyperscalers are cloud service providers; as their name denotes, they have the ability to rapidly scale compute resources from geographically dispersed data centers. Hyperscalers focused on for this study will be Amazon Web Services (AWS), Microsoft Azure, and Google Cloud Platform (GCP) as those are the largest based on current market share and customer base, and adoption. Cloud service models are categorized as public, private, and hybrid. Public refers to a third-party managed service, and private is typically owned and operated by the organization requiring the services, hybrid refers to an entitiy that uses infrastructure and services which traverse both public and private. Some of the prominent cloud service offerings are AWS Elastic Compute Cloud (EC2), Azure Active Directory (AAD), and Google's Big Data Service (BDS) [11][12].

B. *Problem Statement*

The rate of US Federal IT spending on public cloud services has been growing exponentially over the past ten years. Over 10% of the US Federal Government's IT budget is now used for public cloud services which are consumed in a "utility" model [13][14]. Unlike capital expenses for on-premises data center hardware and software, the cost of public cloud services is difficult to quantify and predict. Macroeconomic volatility presents an enhanced socioeconomic risk. A strategy is therefore proposed to ensure diversification through governance.

The research goal is to use systems thinking and systems dynamics methods to establish boundaries of the system under analysis, examine the causal relationships of system elements and propose a cloud sustainability model that is based on principles, not process [15][16][17]. The motivation of this study is to contribute to the body of knowledge towards a significant and timely problem that is beginning to present itself in E-Government and may have far-reaching economic consequences if not adequately addressed.

C. Research Questions

The following are research questions we aspire to answer in this study:

1) What are the endogenous and exogenous boundaries for modeling E-Government consumption of public cloud computing resources?
2) Using a causal structure, how do you model the Federal US Government IT consumption of Public Cloud Services?
3) How can you represent the life cycle of Public Cloud services in a dynamic model?
4) Are there factors that may limit the long-term growth of Cloud service utilization in E-Government?

II. Approach & Methods

The foundational method employed for this study was a systematic literature review. The inclusion and exclusion criteria involved selecting conference papers and scholarly journal papers via major academic search engines such as IEEE Xplore, Academic Search Premiere, and Scopus. The time frame selected was from 2006 to the present as the modern concept of cloud computing is relatively new and was formed alongside the Hyperscaler organizations such as AWS, Microsoft, and Google.

Systems thinking methods are used to identify the primary stakeholders and their endogenous and exogenous boundaries. Causal loop diagrams provide an overview of reinforcing and balancing elements in our analysis. Stock and flow dynamic diagrams are also represented to quantify the accumulation and drainage of elements such as budget amounts. Valves provide us with the rate of inflows and, in our model, connect to the causal loops. By employing a multi-disciplinary approach, the data collected can be observed from multiple angles leading to a more thorough analysis and conceptual understanding of the research.

A. Timeline

In Figure 1, green markers represent the launch dates of Amazon Web Services in 2006, Google Cloud Platform in 2008, and Microsoft Azure in 2010. The pillars in blue represent significant milestones in the public cloud, such as the modern cloud computing concept introduction by then-Google CEO Eric Schmidt. This is followed by AWS's significant expansion in Europe and Asia, which is now gaining global traction for its public cloud services. In 2016 the Gartner magic quadrant was released for infrastructure as a service, with only three companies in the Leadership quadrants showing how far behind the others have fallen.

Events in orange denote the milestones of government public cloud adoption. Changes, such as creating a Federal cloud computing PMO in 2009 and passing the Modernizing Government Technology (MGT) act, allow government agencies to begin to invest in public cloud services. Markers in dark grey show dynamic year-over-year double-digit hyperscaler revenue growth, hitting 81% in 2015. In 2021, the Federal IT budget allocation for the public cloud topped ten billion and exceeded 10% of the total funding. The final red

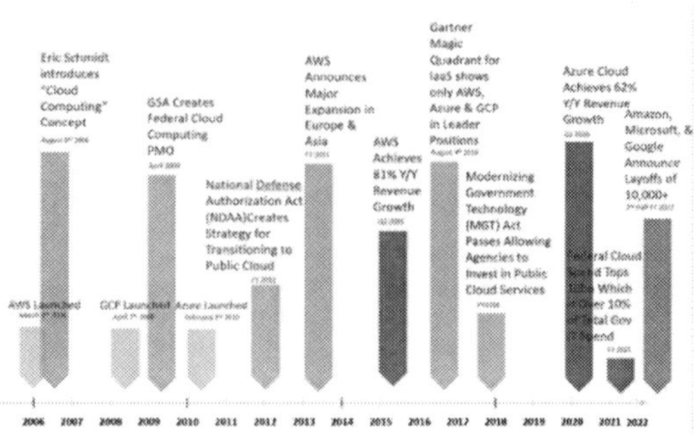

Fig. 1. Timeline.

marker shows the recent downward trend in all three hyperscaler organizations leading to extensive tech industry layoffs.

B. Boundary

In an effort to define the endogenous and exogenous elements, key system stakeholders and orient our study, Figure 2 presents a stakeholder interest map.

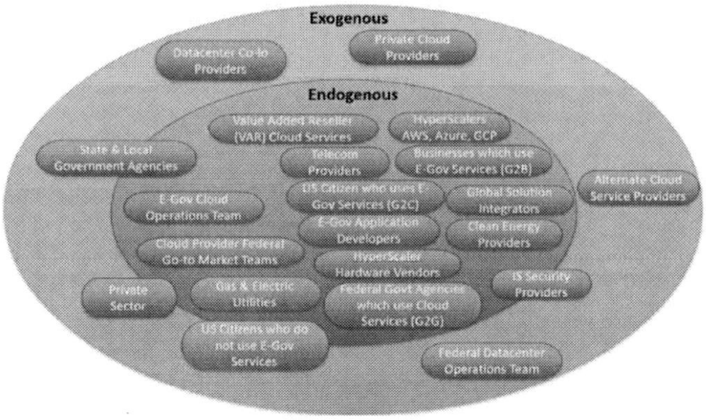

Fig. 2. Stakeholder Interest Map.

Internal to this study are what we consider E-Government primary consumers: citizens, businesses, government employees, and alternate government agencies. Also endogenous in this model are the public cloud operations and customer success teams which partner with value-added resellers to provide professional services and support based on requirement [18]. Utility providers and clean energy partners deliver services that power, cool, and regulate the large tier-four data centers. Exogenous stakeholders include alternate (non-big-three) cloud service providers, Federal data center operations teams, and co-location providers.

Multiple stakeholders straddle endogenous and exogenous boundaries, such as information system security providers, as they serve both the public and private sectors. Also, US citizens who do not use E-Government services still contribute to taxes that fund budgets, so they cannot be entirely removed from the endogenous stakeholder list.

C. Causal Loop

A causal structure model is presented in Figure 3 and focuses on E-Government service development [13][19]. The first stock represents an accumulation of services that are currently in development. The valve following into this stock is the rate of new projects. Out of the E-government services development stock flows a link with a positive polarity to the expected service rejection rate, which is expected based on evaluations of solutions. Connected to service rejection are the approvals, which have negative incoming polarity and a positive one towards the expected increase in operational efficiency. New services typically enhance effectiveness and lead to the next variable, customer satisfaction rate, with a positive incoming polarity. Next is the expected business value of new services, which completes the chain and creates a clockwise balancing loop due to the single negative polarity.

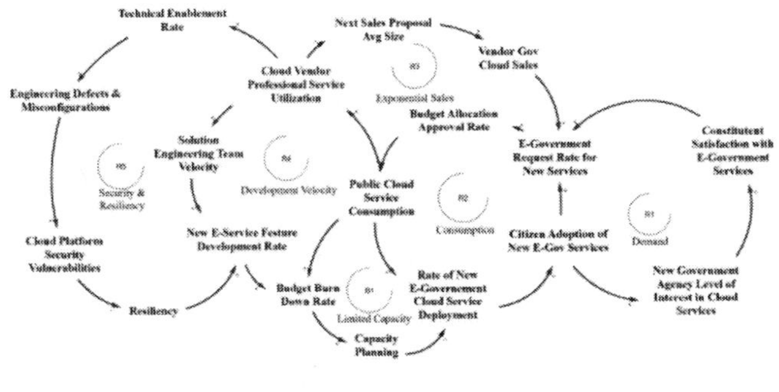

Fig. 3. Causal Loop.

Out of the E-government services, the stock also flows a positive connection to the service development rate valve, which has a negative development delay relationship because any delay can significantly impact our flow. On the model's right side, we have a stock representing E-Government services in production. Out of that stock, there is a positive relationship to the service rejection rate, reducing the IT budget stock down the line. There is a delay in the IT budget in two directions; the arrow on the left is the budgeted IT costs and has a positive polarity towards the expected approvals variable. Flowing in the opposite direction of the IT budget stock is another delay towards the desired new capabilities of the individual government agencies. There is a positive relationship between these new desired capabilities and the demand for new services, which has a negative relationship with the service rejection rate, creating another counter-clockwise balancing loop. The service rejection rate connects to the expected service rejection rate with positive polarity, making our final complete loop another clockwise balancing loop.

Completing the model is a negative polarity from the average life of services to the service decommission rate valve. This value connects to the opposite flow of the rate of new project charters denoting that as services are retired, new services are being formed in their place. The final variables which affect our model are E-Government growth positively connected to the demand for additional resources, and this increased demand having a positive polarity towards the demand for new services.

D. Cloud Diversity Principles

Cloud diversity principles, shown in Figure 4, provide a strategic way that E-Government entities can evaluate the public cloud solutions and make determinations based on principles over process. Principles were selected based on their level of importance and impact as it relates to cloud operating paradigms. These areas were consistently referenced in the literature and related cloud computing case studies hence their inclusion in the framework. A thorough understanding of vendor cost models, including resource consumption, falls under the economical principle. This involves understanding per unit costs, terms of service, and the value chain of public cloud adoption. It is critical to understand how pricing is established to ensure the predictability of spend for budgetary purposes. Interoperability of services and platforms ensures that systems that are already established have a level of integration to the public cloud service, this prevents silos and greater efficiency of operational resources.

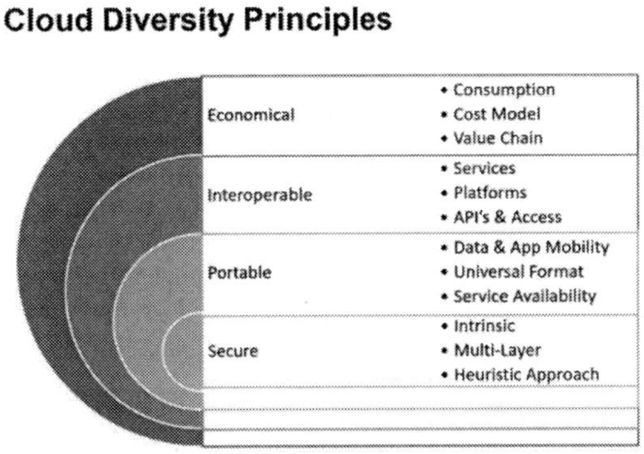

Fig. 4. Cloud Diversity Principles.

The ability to migrate data and workloads to disparate services is a key tenant of the portability principle. Preventing vendor lock-in scenarios and "sticky" service solutions is paramount to ensuring the most cost-effective landing zones can be utilized and open universal formats are adopted. The final principle is security which should be intrinsic to the architecture and follow defense-in-depth tenets. Defense-in-depth refers to the use of multiple security mechanisms such as firewalls, endpoint agents, or intrusion prevention and detection systems deployed in layers on the target system. Heuristics have become increasingly important as the types of cybersecurity threats have grown, the system should have an early detection mechanism and understand anomalous behavior with automated remediation processes.

III. CONCLUSION & FUTURE WORK

E-Government will continue to grow due to the exponential demand for digital services. The next generations will expect government services to be easily accessible via mobile platforms with fast access to data and relevant content. For this reason, public cloud services and their respective capabilities will be necessary to build future iterations of innovative applications and public sector cloud-hosted services. We first set our boundary via a systemigram in Figure 1 and showed the interconnections of these endogenous components. Next, we explored our first causal relationship diagram in Figure 2, which highlighted the multi-dimensional loops and balancing behavior as a result of the stock, flows, and variable linkages. In Figure 3, we leveraged the aging chain and logically segmented the system by the maturity of services through the system. We can model the effect of time on and quantify the rates at which E-Government services get evaluated, moved into a production environment, and finally move towards decommissioning, and replacement [20][21].

Research questions related to the boundary, causal structure, as well as service life-cycle have been addressed via our models. Factors that may limit the long-term growth of cloud services in E-Government should be addressed with a more quantitative model; therefore, any results have a low degree of accuracy; this also holds true for the question around the quantitative significance of factors related to development velocity, budgetary constraints as well as service retirement rates [10]. While we have leveraged multiple models to test our hypotheses, the ones we employed are more basic in nature. This is due to the time allotted for the study as well as research experience with these dynamic tools. To further this research, a greater dive with more profound expertise on the subject would be required to build out the quantitative models that accurately depict this E-Government service adoption and budgeting life-cycle. The data collection process for this research was rudimentary and would yield more accurate results if additional rigor and time were allocated. A literature review with greater depth and acceptance criteria could also bolster the quality of our overall study. Some additional areas of research which could be complementary to this study would be focused on the E-Government application development process, associated toolchains, and possibly enablement methods to understand if more significant outcomes can be achieved through the build-out of a new government innovation lab. This would involve the government operating like a start-up and attracting top-tier technical talent, typically captured by big tech companies. This would be a significant shift based on how government IT operations have traditionally operated but not impossible; it would take a shift in mindset and policy, which is not impossible.

REFERENCES

[1] • *U.S. federal government IT budget 2022 | Statista*, 2022. [Online]. Available: https://www.statista.com/statistics/605501/united-states-federal-it-budget/.

[2] K. A. Torkura, M. I. Sukmana, F. Cheng, and C. Meinel, "CloudStrike: Chaos Engineering for Security and Resiliency in Cloud Infrastructure," *IEEE Access*, vol. 8, pp. 123 044–123 060, 2020, ISSN: 21693536. DOI: 10.1109/ACCESS.2020.3007338.

[3] J. Lu, J. Sun, R. Xiao, and S. Jin, "DIFCS: A Secure Cloud Data Sharing Approach Based on Decentralized Information Flow Control," *Computers and Security*, vol. 117, p. 102 678, 2022, ISSN: 01674048. DOI: 10.1016/j.cose.2022.102678. [Online]. Available: https://doi.org/10.1016/j.cose.2022.102678.

[4] P. L. Sun, C. Y. Ku, and D. H. Shih, "An implementation framework for E-Government 2.0," *Telematics and Informatics*, vol. 32, no. 3, pp. 504–520, 2015, ISSN: 07365853. DOI: 10.1016/j.tele.2014.12.003. [Online]. Available: http://dx.doi.org/10.1016/j.tele.2014.12.003.

[5] A. M. Al Khouri, "An Innovative Approach for E-Government Transformation," *International Journal of Managing Value and Supply Chains*, vol. 2, no. 1, pp. 22–43, 2011, ISSN: 22307966. DOI: 10.5121/ijmvsc.2011.2102.

[6] F. M. Al-Balushi, M. Bahari, and A. A. Rahman, "Defining e-Government integration and its objective: A systematic literature review," *2016 3rd International Conference on Computer and Information Sciences, ICCOINS 2016 - Proceedings*, pp. 13–18, 2016. DOI: 10.1109/ICCOINS.2016.7783181.

[7] E. J. Ng'Eno, "Embracing e-Government in service delivery and business to people through libraries: A case for Kenya," *2010 IST-Africa*, pp. 1–9, 2010.

[8] E. P. Purnomo and K. Hubacek, "Management of commons with a proper way: A critical review Hardin's essay on the tragedy of commons," *ICEEA 2010 - 2010 International Conference on Environmental Engineering and Applications, Proceedings*, no. Iceea, pp. 4–7, 2010. DOI: 10.1109/ICEEA.2010.5596078.

[9] D. Sagarik, P. Chansukree, W. Cho, and E. Berman, "E-government 4.0 in Thailand: The role of central agencies," *Information Polity*, vol. 23, no. 3, pp. 343–353, 2018, ISSN: 18758754. DOI: 10.3233/IP-180006.

[10] V. R. Prybutok, X. Zhang, and S. D. Ryan, "Evaluating leadership, IT quality, and net benefits in an e-government environment," *Information and Management*, vol. 45, no. 3, pp. 143–152, 2008, ISSN: 03787206. DOI: 10.1016/j.im.2007.12.004.

[11] H. Zhang, "Analysis of the impact of cloud computing technology to e-government performance evaluation," *Proceedings - 2nd IEEE International Conference on Mobile Cloud Computing, Services, and Engineering, MobileCloud 2014*, pp. 295–298, 2014. DOI: 10.1109/MobileCloud.2014.45.

[12] A. A. Memon, C. Wang, M. R. Naeem, M. Aamir, and M. Ayoob, "Cloud government-a proposed solution to better serve the nation," *Proceedings of 2014 International Conference on Cloud Computing and Internet of Things, CCIOT 2014*, no. Cciot, pp. 39–44, 2014. DOI: 10.1109/CCIOT.2014.7062502.

[13] M. Saeri, M. M. Lotfi, and M. R. Mazidi, "A Causal Loop Diagram to Analyze Various Long-Term Effects of PV Integration into Power Systems," *ICEE 2019 - 27th Iranian Conference on Electrical Engineering*, pp. 852–855, 2019. DOI: 10.1109/IranianCEE.2019.8786514.

[14] N. Ghaffarzadegan and R. C. Larson, "SD meets OR: a new synergy to address policy problems," *System Dynamics Review*, vol. 34, no. 1-2, pp. 327–353, 2018, ISSN: 10991727. DOI: 10.1002/sdr.1598.

[15] M. Mansouri and A. Mostashari, "A systemic approach to governance in extended enterprise systems," *2010 IEEE International Systems Conference Proceedings, SysCon 2010*, pp. 311–316, 2010. DOI: 10.1109/SYSTEMS.2010.5482432.

[16] J. Lu, J. Sun, R. Xiao, and S. Jin, "DIFCS: A Secure Cloud Data Sharing Approach Based on Decentralized Information Flow Control," *Computers and Security*, vol. 117, p. 102 678, 2022, ISSN: 01674048. DOI: 10.1016/j.cose.2022.102678. [Online]. Available: https://doi.org/10.1016/j.cose.2022.102678.

[17] M. Mansouri, B. Sauser, and J. Boardman Dr., "Applications of systems thinking for resilience study in maritime transportation system of systems," *2009 IEEE International Systems Conference Proceedings*, pp. 211–217, 2009. DOI: 10.1109/SYSTEMS.2009.4815800.

[18] J. Sangki, "Vision of future e-government via new e-government maturity model: Based on Korea's e-government practices," *Telecommunications Policy*, vol. 42, no. 10, pp. 860–871, 2018, ISSN: 03085961. DOI: 10.1016/j.telpol.2017.12.002. [Online]. Available: https://doi.org/10.1016/j.telpol.2017.12.002.

[19] G. Haghighat and N. Hosseinichimeh, "Why Organizations Fail to Reflect on Experiences: Insights from a Causal Loop Diagram of Reflection on Experience," *IEEE Engineering Management Review*, vol. 49, no. 1, pp. 81–96, 2021, ISSN: 19374178. DOI: 10.1109/EMR.2020.3045012.

[20] M. J. Ahn and S. Bretschneider, "Politics of E-Government: E-Government and the Political Control of Bureaucracy," *Public Administration Review*, vol. 71, no. 3, pp. 414–424, 2011, ISSN: 00333352. DOI: 10.1111/j.1540-6210.2011.02225.x.

[21] S. D. Ryan, X. Zhang, V. R. Prybutok, and J. H. Sharp, "Leadership and Knowledge Management in an E-Government Environment," *Administrative Sciences*, vol. 2, no. 1, pp. 63–81, 2012, ISSN: 2076-3387. DOI: 10.3390/admsci2010063.

The Unintended Effects of Medical Software on Clinical Decisions and Patient Safety: A System Viewpoint

Farah Elkourdi
School of Systems and Enterprises
Stevens Institute of Technology
Hoboken, NJ 07030
e-mail: felkourd@stevens.edu

Onur Asan
School of Systems and Enterprises
Stevens Institute of Technology
Hoboken, NJ 07030
e-mail: oasan@stevens.edu

Mo Mansouri
School of Systems and Enterprises
Stevens Institute of Technology
Hoboken, NJ 07030
e-mail: mo.mansouri@stevens.edu

Abstract—**Integrating medical software into the healthcare system began as a way to reduce medical errors and simplify procedures. However, medical software-related errors have been a source of concern for both physicians and patients. Software-related medical errors have affected clinical decisions, which threaten patient safety. This paper explores the potential sources of unintended negative consequences associated with medical software. We used systems thinking methods to explore the relationship between software-related errors and their overall impact. We also developed insights into how to improve patient safety by eliminating software-related medical errors system-wide.**

Keywords- Medical Software; Healthcare; System Thinking; Clinical Decisions; Patient Safety; Medical Errors; Human Factors.

I. INTRODUCTION

According to the World Health Organization, patient safety is a healthcare discipline that emerged with the evolving complexity of healthcare systems and the resulting rise of patient harm in healthcare facilities, which aims to prevent and reduce risks, errors, and harm that occur to patients during the provision of health care [1]. Patients cannot always notice the consequence of medical software, although it is a vital component of the healthcare system impacting patient safety. Medical software was integrated into healthcare to assist physicians in areas including managing patients' data, improving care coordination, and proper diagnosis. There are several types of medical software used by physicians, such as Electronic Health Records (EHR), E-prescriptions, and Medical diagnosis software. Medical software can enhance the quality of patient care, diminish paper workload, and reduce unnecessary medical tests [2].

Over time, the healthcare system gradually shifted toward integrating medical software. It started in the 1960s when beliefs began to arise around computer technology holding promises for improved decision-making by clinicians [3]. Software development started to evolve over years with noticeable expansion in the healthcare industry. In 2003, both the public and private sectors took major steps to ensure that EHRs would be a component of medical offices within five to eight years [3]. Nowadays, medical software is adapted and widely used by physicians in the healthcare field.

However, medical errors are a serious public health problem and the third-leading cause of death [4]. There are problems associated with healthcare Information Technology (IT) that can disrupt care delivery and harm patients [5]. From this standpoint, what factors have led medical software to become a source of harm despite its primary objective to improve patient safety? Systems and Software Engineering contribute to the advancement and improvement of healthcare delivery and its safety [6]. In this paper, we will analyze, from a system viewpoint, the reasons behind causing the unintended consequences of medical software on clinical decisions and patient safety. A human being usually reacts to immediate circumstances, but it is more difficult to analyze how our previous actions and decisions may influence a specific situation in the future [7]. We will use system thinking methods to identify the relationship between events and potential improvements.

The rest of this paper is organized as follows. Section II describes the potential sources of software medical errors in healthcare. Section III describes the stakeholders' perspectives on medical software development. Section IV addresses some of the unintended consequences related to medical software that affect clinical decisions, patient care, and safety. Section V discusses the conclusion of integrating medical software into healthcare systems.

II. POTENTIAL SOURCES OF UNINTENDED CONSEQUENCES

Medical software is a computer program intended for use in the diagnosis, cure, mitigation, treatment, or prevention of disease, or intended to affect the structure or any function of the body of humans; or used in the production or control of drugs, devices, data, or other uses in medical diagnosis or treatment [8]. Implementing software into the healthcare system might produce possible unforeseen consequences due to the complexity of the healthcare system and various stakeholders, such as the development team, policymakers, and physicians. The successful implementation of medical software involves assessing multiple aspects, such as its interaction with the people, processes, and culture of the organization to deliver safe care for patients and a more satisfying work experience for clinicians and staff [9].

Figure 1 shows the potential sources of unintended consequences related to medical software in the healthcare system. Eliminating the negative consequences of medical software and identifying their potential sources requires understanding the subsystems' interaction. IT development teams should concentrate on developing reliable software, especially for critical industries, such as the healthcare field. The development of reliable software consists of a series of phases that shape the software system's complexity. The phases start with requirements and end when the product reaches the market in addition to applying verification and validation techniques throughout the different phases [10]. The development process involves difficulties in managing the medical software without negatively affecting patient safety, privacy, and security. As a result, regulations were enacted and evolved for medical software development to ensure patient safety and protect patients' data. For example, U.S. Food and Drug Administration (FDA) intends to apply its regulatory oversight to the medical device software functions whose functionality could pose a risk to a patient's safety if the device were not to function as intended [11]. Besides, organizations that use medical records have to follow privacy and security regulations for managing patient information in the healthcare industry [12]. The impact of regulations and policies on medical software is presented in green arrows in Figure 1.

Medical software risks can arise from flaws in the software itself, introduced during development, unintended consequences, or the physician's use of the software [13]. Software medical errors caused in a hospital environment involve workload, stress, and fatigue integrated with usability issues, such as poor software interface design, and reliability issues, such as functional errors [4][5][14]. Software quality attributes are the nonfunctional requirements that define the software system from the user's point of view, and it represents a critical component of the software system to achieve the field objectives. Medical software quality attributes include reliability, usability, safety, privacy, and security. In healthcare, poor software quality may have safety implications; for example, using an electronic prescribing system that corrupts data about the dose of a prescription, or a patient management system that stores incorrect information about the criticality of the condition [13]. The blue arrows in Figure 1 present the impact of medical software quality on the healthcare environment.

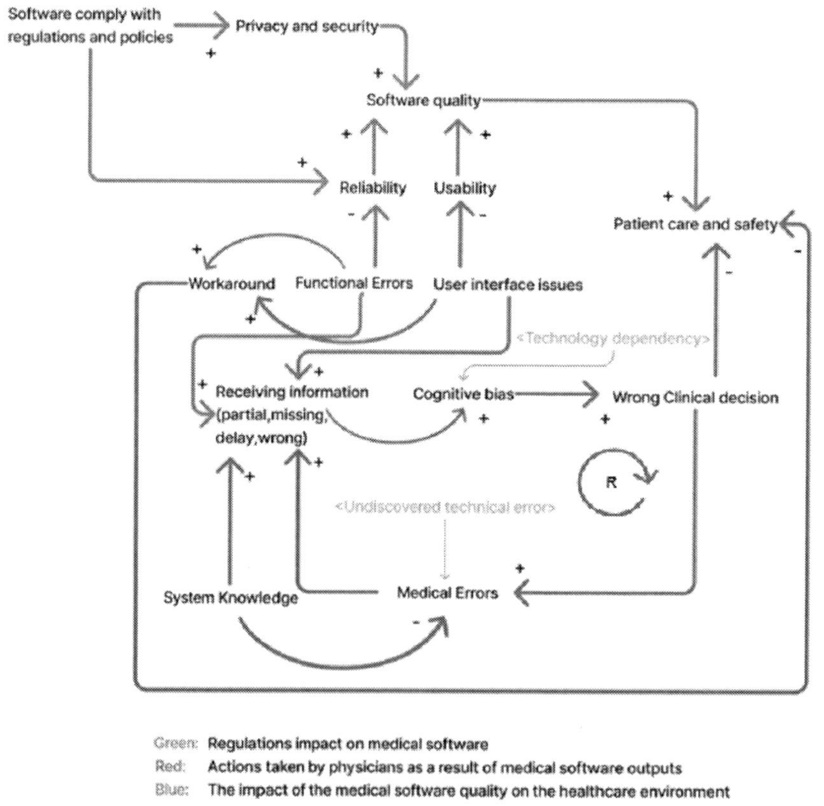

Figure 1. Causal loop presents the potential sources of software medical errors

The healthcare field is a dynamic and complex environment. The physicians might be under psychological (anxiety, grief, and guilt) and cognitive (compassion dissatisfaction, burnout, and stress) pressure [4]. When developers make mistakes, the consequences may not be foreseen for a long time; the physicians have to respond rapidly although they are under substantial workload pressures, and they may not understand that their problems are triggered by faulty code [15]. Technical issues could result in physicians receiving wrong, incomplete, delayed, or missing information [5]. Physicians might use workarounds to overcome technical issues. Workaround caused the system to be used in a way that it is not intended to be used which might cause medical errors [14]. Hazards might turn into risks causing harm generated by the physicians due to the limited amount of knowledge known about the software system. Knowledge refers to understanding the system's functionalities. Physicians might not use some functions due to a lack of knowledge and proper training, which could reduce the productivity and efficiency of the healthcare system [14]. The workflows in the healthcare environment have complexity in task structures as physicians manage multiple competing demands under resource constraints, and from psychology, the complexity leads to cognitive load and error [16]. Besides, human cognition, its limitations, and reliance on heuristics can affect human decision-making processes, which can alter how humans weigh the importance of data when making a decision [16]. Unexpected errors will always be a part of the medical system due to the universal nature of human fallibility and technology [4]. The red arrows in Figure 1 present physicians' actions as a result of medical software outputs. The key objective is to eliminate the potential sources of the negative consequences to deliver a high care quality in clinical decisions and support patient safety.

III. DIFFERENT PERSPECTIVES AND VALUES

In Figure 2, we demonstrate the different perspectives of multiple stakeholders in the system. The four perspectives are human factors in developing software that adapts to the healthcare field, meeting deadlines for business market races and competitions, considering the technical aspect to develop stable software, and applying regulations to protect patients' safety, data privacy, and security. The ideal point for producing medical software is to maintain in the middle to observe the full picture that is balancing between all four different values without drifting to one aspect. For example, considering the software functionality technical aspect from one perspective will result in losing other values, such as human factors from the physicians' perspective. The primary objective should be the patients' right to provide safe, reliable, and patient-centered care [4].

A. *Policymakers' perspective*

Policymakers have established regulations to ensure the safety and privacy of patient data. Developers must consider government regulations, human factors, and stable functionalities while developing medical software. Health Insurance Portability and Accountability Act (HIPAA) is a federal law that protects sensitive patient health information from being revealed without the patient's permission or knowledge [17]. For example, electronic health record systems are required to have audit functions to detect the identity of the users accessing the system [18]. The violations of regulations may not only cause the disclosure of patients' sensitive information, but also can cause no-tolerance penalties and termination to the healthcare providers [18].

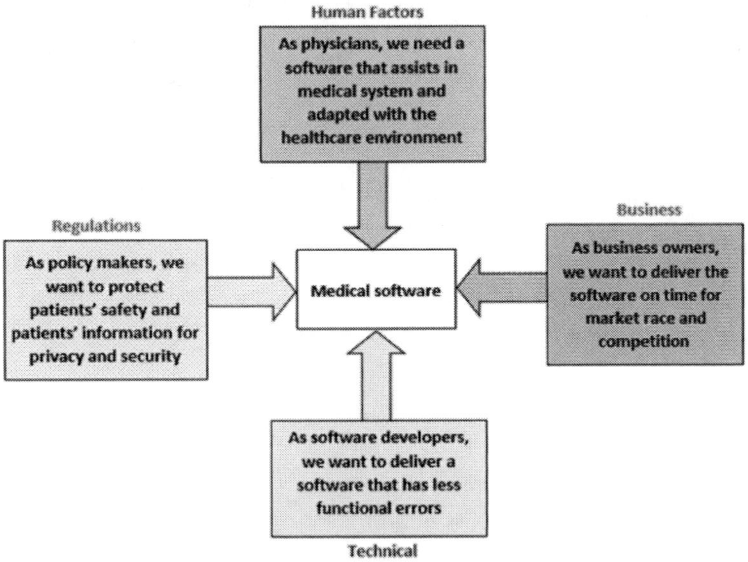

Figure 2. Different perspectives of multiple stakeholders in the system

B. Technical versus business perspective

Software developers are concerned with avoiding functional errors. As a result of the industry's race to market [19], software developers may be under pressure to meet deadlines and market competition, which might cause spaghetti code that is more prone to errors. Spaghetti code is unstructured code programmed by software developers and can be caused by taking shortcuts to meet deadlines. Delivering unstructured code might result in a chain of errors that will appear when physicians are using the system. More errors will start to appear while fixing one error due to the spaghetti unstructured code [19]. This concludes to a complex software system that is difficult to track, maintain or extend and accordingly results in a prone code to errors. Healthcare organizations must collaborate with their software vendors to monitor and optimize the used technology to help them identify, measure, and improve the quality and safety of the care provided [20].

C. Human factors perspective

Physicians focus on having medical software that would allow for the best patient care and adapted to their workflow in healthcare. Medical errors may occur if the medical software development team fails to consider human factors perspectives when developing a stable software system for a healthcare environment. For example, developing a drop-down menu listing 86 options that are irrelevant for a specified patient might cause physicians to make errors by clicking on the wrong dose or form [19]. This could have an impact on clinical decisions and patient safety. In this case, the development team did not deliver a functional error but missed the other values from different perspectives.

Human factors for medical software involve designing user interfaces so that physicians can complete their tasks without making errors that might affect patient safety. There are some approaches to include human factors in user interface development, such as hiring human factors engineers or psychologists directly into development teams, placing a development group under the leadership of a human factors professional, or forming an educational center in which software engineers learn about human factors approaches [21]. Effective human factors methods could be applied routinely and during the software development life cycle phases, which could minimize the negative unintended consequences and reduce the chance of errors [22].

Errors and poor user interfaces might interfere with receiving the information and lead to errors when making decisions [5]. To address patient safety that arises from human error as well as other sources, systems, and software engineering attention must increasingly focus on continuously creating robust, reliable, and dependable applications and infrastructure focused on addressing needs at the point of delivery of care [6]. Medical software containing software functional errors or design issues is causing hazards in the healthcare environment. Suppose the physician did not discover the functional errors or the design issues in the early stage. In that case, it will turn into a risk that will negatively affect the clinical decisions and patient safety, as shown in Figure 3. If the physician detects the error in the early stage before it turns into a medical error, it will cause a workload to work around the error. However, it will still be a hazard caused by the workarounds that might affect patients' safety, as mentioned in Figure 3.

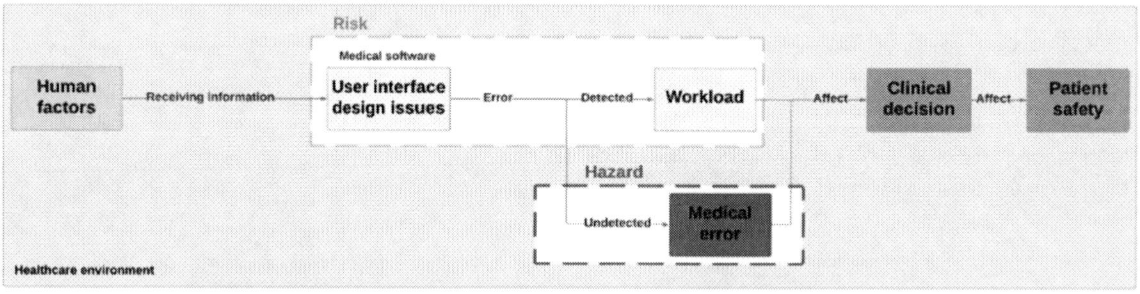

Figure 3. The impact of human factors and medical software on clinical decision and patient safety

IV. Some unintended consequences related to medical software affect clinical decisions, patient care, and safety

According to the "potential sources of unintended consequences" section, some unintended consequences caused by medical software affect the clinical decision and patient safety, such as causing new types of errors in healthcare, producing new/more workload on physicians, and technology dependency in taking decisions. Commission errors are the most commonly reported software medical errors in healthcare generated by wrong data entry, selection from dropdown menus, and file uploads [5]. The effects of it cause errors and delays in clinical decision including medication administration errors and failure to follow up test results [5].

Medical software may increase the hazards in the healthcare field and cause new types of errors due to the doctor's computer interaction or functional errors generated during the software development. Software developers must optimize the design of human-computer interfaces because interface design issues cause many medical errors [23]. The dependency on medical software is one of the consequences that could have a negative impact. If the system is down, physicians should ensure that basic medical care can continuously be provided in the absence of technology [18]. Furthermore, medical software could generate new or more work for physicians as unintended consequences. Accordingly, developers should enhance the user interface to reduce the collection of redundant information, display relevant information in logical locations and reduce the amount of typing [23].

V. Conclusion

As healthcare systems continue to rely more heavily on medical software, it is crucial to evaluate their effectiveness and safety. In this paper, we discuss the potential sources of negative consequences generated by integrating medical software into the healthcare field from a systems perspective. Our discussion reveals that the challenges rely on applying a complex system "the medical software" into another complex system "the healthcare" system. We started with the primary reasons for integrating medical software in the healthcare field and its evolution over the years. We demonstrate the interaction between software developers, policymakers, and healthcare providers. Besides, introducing the different values and perspectives in delivering medical software. Our objective is to identify potential sources of unintended consequences in order to eliminate negative outcomes.

The system stakeholders must collaborate and communicate effectively to ensure that the medical software is developed and implemented to prioritize patient safety and care. This requires collaboration between healthcare providers and software developers to provide continuous user feedback and develop a user-centered design. Consequently, medical software can effectively support healthcare providers in delivering and improving outcomes.

References

[1] W. H. Organization, "Patient Safety," World Health Organization, 13 September 2019. [Online]. Available: https://www.who.int/news-room/fact-sheets/detail/patient-safety. [Accessed 21 March 2023].

[2] healthit.gov, "Advantages of Electronic Health Records," healthit.gov, 8 March 2022. [Online]. Available: https://www.healthit.gov/faq/what-are-advantages-electronic-health-records. [Accessed 21 March 2023].

[3] E. Ambinder, "A History of the Shift Toward Full Computerization of Medicine," American Society of Clinical Oncolog, vol. 1, no. 2, pp. 54-56, 2005.

[4] O. Ozeke, V. Ozeke, O. Coskun, and I. I. Budakoglu, "Second victims in health care: current perspectives," Advances in Medical Education and Practice, vol. 10, pp. 593–603, 2019.

[5] M. O. Kim, E. Coiera, and F. Magrabi, "Problems with health information technology and their effects on care delivery and patient outcomes: a systematic review," Journal of the American Medical Informatics Association, vol. 24, no. 2, pp. 246-250, 2017.

[6] R. A. Schrenker, "Software engineering for future healthcare and clinical systems," Computer, vol. 39, no. 4, pp. 26 - 32, 2006.

[7] H. Sibo-Ingrid, G. Celis-David, and S. Liou, "Systems Thinking: a paradigm for advancing technology to enhance humanity," in IEEE International Conference on Orange Technologies (ICOT), Nusa Dua, Bali, 2018, pp. 1-6, doi: 10.1109/ICOT.2018.8705910.

[8] P. Schneider and M. Hines, "Classification of medical software," in Symposium on Applied Computing, Arkansas, 1990, pp. 20-27, doi: 10.1109/SOAC.1990.82134.

[9] Healthit.gov, "Implementing Health IT," [Online]. Available: https://www.healthit.gov/topic/safety/implementing-health-it. [Accessed 21 March 2023].

[10] D. Leggingwell and B. Norman, "Software quality in medical devices-a top-down approach," in Computer-Based Medical Systems-Proceedings of the Sixth Annual IEEE Symposium, Michigan, 1993, pp. 307-311, doi: 10.1109/CBMS.1993.263001.

[11] FDA, "Policy for Device Software Functions and Mobile Medical Applications," U.S. Food & Drug, September 2022. [Online]. Available: https://www.fda.gov/regulatory-information/search-fda-guidance-documents/policy-device-software-functions-and-mobile-medical-applications [Accessed 21 March 2023].

[12] D. Baumer, J. B. Earp, and F. C. Payton, "Privacy of medical records: IT implications of HIPAA," ACM SIGCAS Computers and Society, vol. 30, no. 4, pp. 40–47, 2000.

[13] G. Despotou, S. White, T. Kelly, and M. Ryan, "Introducing safety cases for health IT," in ICSE Workshop on Software Engineering in Health Care, SEHC, Zurich, 2012, pp. 44-50, doi: 10.1109/SEHC.2012.6227010.

[14] L. Salahuddin and Z. Ismail, "Antecedents for safety in health IT: An exploratory investigation," in Proceedings of

the 6th International Conference on Information Technology and Multimedia, Putrajaya, 2014, pp. 38-43, doi: 10.1109/ICIMU.2014.7066600.

[15] H. Thimbleby, "Inside Medical Software: When Programming Errors Cost Lives," ITNow, vol. 60, no. 2, pp. 50-52, 2018.

[16] E. Coiera, J. Ash, and M. Berg, "The Unintended Consequences of Health Information Technology Revisited," Yearb Med Inform, vol. 25, pp. 163–169, 2016.

[17] CDC, "Health Insurance Portability and Accountability Act of 1996 (HIPAA)," Centers for Disease Control and Prevention, 27 June 2022. [Online]. Available: https://www.cdc.gov/phlp/publications/topic/hipaa.html#:~:text=The%20Health%20Insurance%20Portability%20and,the%20patient's%20consent%20or%20knowledge [Accessed 21 March 2023].

[18] N. Menachemi and T. H. Collum, "Benefits and drawbacks of electronic health record systems," Risk Manag Healthc Policy, vol. 4, pp. 47-55, 2011.

[19] F. Schulte and E. Fry "Death By 1,000 Clicks: Where Electronic Health Records Went Wrong," KHN, 18 MARCH 2019. [Online]. Available: https://khn.org/news/death-by-a-thousand-clicks/. [Accessed 21 March 2023].

[20] D. F. Sittig et al., "Current Challenges in Health Information Technology-related Patient Safety," Health Informatics J., vol. 26, pp. 181-189, 2020.

[21] J. Grudin, J. Carroll, S. Ehrlich, M. Grisham, and H. Hersh, "Integrating human factors and software development," in CHI '88: Proceedings of the SIGCHI Conference on Human Factors in Computing Systems, Washington D.C., 1988, pp. 157–159.

[22] A. Kushniruk, C. Nohr, and E. Borycki, "Human Factors for More Usable and Safer Health Information Technology: Where Are We Now and Where do We Go from Here?," Yearb Med Inform, pp. 120–125, 2016.

[23] E. M. Campbell, D. F. Sittig, J. S. Ash, K. P. Guappone, and R. H. Dykstra, "Types of Unintended Consequences Related to Computerized Provider Order Entry," J Am Med Inform Assoc., vol. 13, no. 5, pp. 547–556, 2006.

Transformative Computing for Cyber-Security Protocols

Lidia Ogiela
AGH University of Krakow
30 Mickiewicza Ave, 30-059 Kraków, Poland
e-mail: logiela@agh.edu.pl

Marek R. Ogiela
AGH University of Krakow
30 Mickiewicza Ave, 30-059 Kraków, Poland
e-mail: mogiela@agh.edu.pl

Abstract—**This paper will discuss the main techniques based on transformative solutions, dedicated to data protection and security. Transformative computing is designed to collect and analyze data obtained from various sources, taking into account their updates and changes. The analysis of data obtained from various sources is possible by using linguistic and semantic techniques to describe and interpret data in order to properly extract information contained in large data sets. Linguistic techniques guarantee the proper description of the analyzed data and the selection of relevant information in a given analysis process. These processes allow for proper data protection both in common use systems and in cyberspace.**

Keywords-Transformative computing; linguistic techniques; cyber-security protocols.

I. INTRODUCTION

Transformative computing methodology is dedicated to the implementation of complex and large data sets processing, obtained from various sources, at various times, recorded by various recorders [2][4][5]. Thus, these are calculations that process different data sets. Their diversity allows to obtain information of great importance for the data processing process. Determining the meaning is possible thanks to the use of linguistic techniques in the process of interpretation and inference. Linguistic techniques dedicated to the tasks of meaningful interpretation of data allow to obtain information that can significantly affect the process of automatic data understanding [6][7]. Data understanding processes, on the other hand, are an innovative solution in the field of constructing data protection and security protocols. The main area of application of the discussed solutions are cryptographic threshold schemes, intended for data security tasks through their sharing [1][3][7].

The novelty presented in this paper is the possibility of dedicating transformative techniques to the processes of data security for cyber-security protocols.

The rest of the paper is structured as follows. In Section II, we introduce the concept of the Transformative Computing paradigm. In Section III, a security protocol based on linguistic threshold schemes will be described. Finally, we conclude the work in Section IV.

II. TRANSFORMATIVE COMPUTING METHODOLOGY

Transformative computing methodology is used to implement complex computational processes. Their important aspect is that the data on the basis of which the calculations are made, may come from various sources recording information in real time. An important advantage of such computing is therefore the ability to combine data sets of different nature, size and format. This is possible thanks to the use of techniques that are primarily used to extract important (from the analysis point of view) information that is important for the process of description and inference. This stage is carried out on the basis of the use of linguistic techniques in the process of describing the interpreted data.

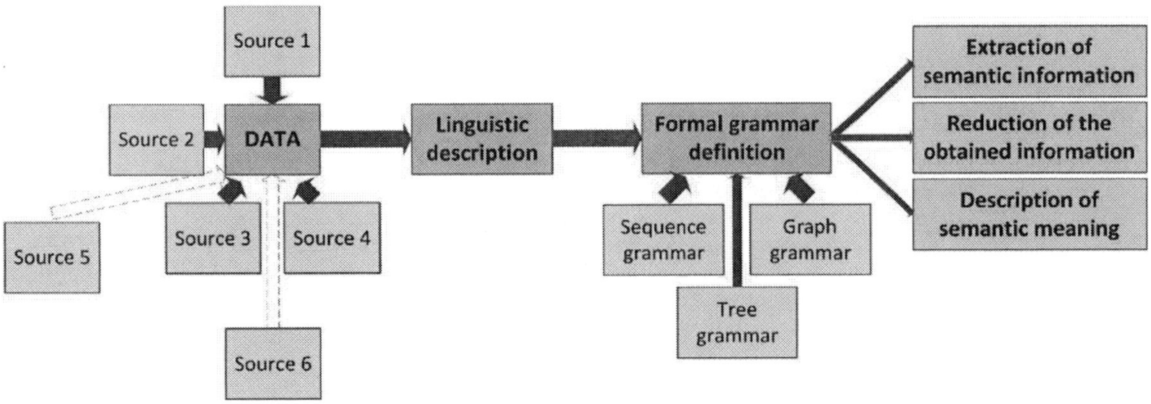

Figure 1. Transformative computing methodology.

Linguistic techniques allow the extraction of semantic information contained in data sets. This information is used to describe the importance of the analyzed collections and thus allows for a significant reduction of the obtained information. At this stage, the method of description the analyzed data is also selected, using linguistic techniques of data interpretation in the form of formal grammars. The choice of the right grammar rules depends on the type of data for which the analysis is carried out, but it is focused on the choice of sequence, tree or graph grammar. A schematic representation of the transformation calculation process is shown in Figure 1.

III. CYBER-SECURITY PROTOCOLS

Data security protocols based on the use of linguistic techniques for the proper extraction of data constituting secret information that may be subject to confidentiality processes are gaining more and more importance. Their main task is to protect and secure confidential, secret or strategic data. High-priority data protection are in classical cryptographic systems, but also in the cyber security. The idea behind the new generation of solutions is the ability to use effective methods of securing data with a high security priority. A new solution is the possibility of using linguistic techniques in threshold schemes to provide a semantic description of a shared secret and the possibility of splitting data obtained from transformative computing. An important advantage of this solution is the acquisition of relevant data with semantic meaning while eliminating irrelevant or low-importance data. In addition, this solution allows the use of linguistic techniques in the process of dividing a secret between a specific group of secret keepers. At the same time, the semantic analysis of the secret may constitute its part as an element subject to secrecy. The method of choosing the optimal data protection protocol takes place at the stage of defining the threshold scheme that is to be used to implement the data protection process (Figure 2).

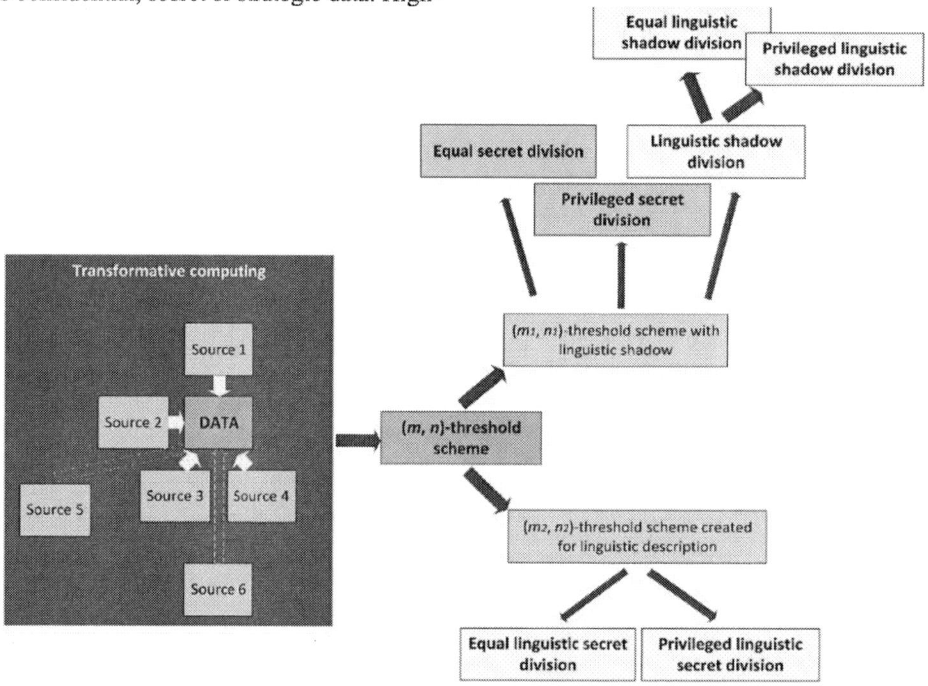

Figure 2. Transformative computing for linguistic threshold schemes in security protocols.

Linguistic techniques included in the data protection process based on threshold schemes, can be used in data protection processes in cyber security. Their advantage is high flexibility resulting from the possibility of selecting data recording sources for the implementation of transformative computing, the use of universal secret description techniques using linguistic methods, and the use of linguistic threshold schemes that guarantee an accurate description of the secured data enriched with elements of semantic description.

Data security protocols dedicated to cyber security guarantee high security and the possibility of their continuous modification due to emerging changes in procedures, opportunities and threats, both external and internal. The threshold schemes proposed in this paper, based on transformative computing methodology and semantic inference techniques, guarantee a high level of data protection. Transformative computing combined with linguistic reasoning techniques can be applied to multi-level structures, which makes it much easier to manage them from different levels of the entire process and structure. Such a solution can therefore be effectively used in cyber security, where data security processes are carried out at various levels. The universality of the presented solution results from the use of transformative computing techniques in the process of obtaining and processing data, which constitute information of a secret nature, results from the possibility of extracting the semantic meaning only for relevant data, and from the possibility of constructing threshold schemes in order to divide the secret along with its semantic description (contained in the additional secret shadow) between the secret trustees.

IV. Conclusions

This paper presents an innovative approach to the process of securing data using linguistic threshold schemes, in which semantic information presenting the meaning of the secret plays an important role. The linguistic description of the secret is the result of data processing based on transformation techniques that allow the collection and processing of various data sets from different data recorders. The universality of the discussed solutions allows for their wide application, especially in cyber security.

Acknowledgment

This work has been partially supported by the funds of the Polish Ministry of Education and Science assigned to AGH University of Krakow. The research project was supported by the program „Excellence initiative – research university" for the AGH University of Krakow.

References

[1] M. Biro, A. Mashkoor, and J. Sametinger, "Safety and security of cyber-physical systems," J. of Softw.-Evol. and Proc. e2522, 2022, doi: 10.1002/smr.2522.

[2] S. Gil at al., "Transformative effects of IoT, Blockchain and Artificial Intelligence on cloud computing: Evolution, vision, trends and open challenges," Inter. of Things. Vol.8, paper 100118, 2019.

[3] A. Menezes, P. van Oorschot, and S. Vanstone, "Handbook of Applied Cryptography." CRC Press, Waterloo, 2001.

[4] Y. Moustafa and F. Kawsar, "Transformative computing and communication," Computer. Vol. 52 (7), pp. 12-14, 2019.

[5] L. Ogiela, "Transformative computing in advanced data analysis processes in the cloud," Inf. Process. Manage. Vol. 57(5), paper 102260, 2020.

[6] M. R. Ogiela, L. Ogiela, and U. Ogiela, "Biometric methods for advanced strategic data sharing protocols,". In: 2015 9th International Conference on Innovative Mobile and Internet Services in Ubiquitous Computing IMIS 2015, pp. 179–183, 2015, doi: 10.1109/IMIS.2015.29.

[7] M. R. Ogiela and L. Ogiela, "Cognitive cryptography techniques for intelligent information management," Int. J. of Inf. Manage. 40, pp. 21-27, 2018, doi: 10.1016/j.ijinfomgt.2018.01.011.

Operational Management Using Wake-on-LAN

Yeongkwun Kim
School of Computer Sciences
Western Illinois University
Macomb IL, USA
email:Y-Kim2@wiu.edu

Injoo Kim
Department of Computer &
Information Science
East-West University
Chicago IL, USA
email: injoo@eastwest.edu

Abstract - **Remote access is a valuable way to access network resources. Wake-on-LAN (WoL) is a well-known technology commonly used for external remote access. In this work, we implement an operational supporting system to perform key operations such as security checks including virus scanning, software modifications/updates, amongst others. Such functions are all dependent on WoL to access remote systems.**

Keywords-operational management; virus scan; remote login; WoL.

I. INTRODUCTION

The WoL (Wake-on-LAN) has widespread use as a networking protocol that enables clients to wake up all computer systems remotely [1]. It allows administrators to perform system maintenance even if the user has turned off the computer. Appropriately applied, it is valuable for administrative activities such as security patch delivery and framework maintenance as well as for diminishing overall energy utilization. Since it permits administrators to turn on computers remotely, turning off computers while they are not being used does not have any negative effects on system management. It might be particularly helpful for academic institutions or organizations/companies with huge networks to have the option to turn on computers remotely, where the option to turn on all computers within a reasonable timeframe is not viable. WoL is an independent platform, requiring explicit adjustments of the hardware and software to operate appropriately. Most desktop hardware and operating systems such as Microsoft Windows, Mac OS X, and Linux support WoL. In this paper, we present the preliminary findings of our implementation of the operational support system based on the WoL. The rest of this paper is organized as follows. Section II describes related work, Section III describes the WoL, and Section IV addresses the network setup. Section V draws the conclusion and briefly indicates future work.

II. RELATED WORK

Stefanovic et al. [1] used WoL to save time on business processes by turning on and having computers ready for employees when they arrive. Depending on the working hours of each employee, they measured how much the machines used the network. Although they did make use of remote access, they did show that it was possible to turn on users' computers depending on the working hours of each employee. This provides important foundation for possible improvements that can be made by enabling remote access.

III. WAKE-ON-LAN

WoL [2]-[4] is implemented utilizing an extraordinary network message called a magic packet. A magic packet has the MAC address of the destination computer. The listening computer waits for a magic packet routed to it and afterward initiates the system wake-up. The magic packet is sent on the data link or layer 2 in the OSI (Open System Interconnection) model and communicated to all NICs (Network Interface Cards) utilizing the network broadcast address. In order for WoL to function properly, the MAC address of the destination computer is required. The MAC (Medium Access Control) address can be distinguished on a nearby local network by utilizing simple commands, such as, ipconfig/ ifconfig. It is difficult to track down the MAC addresses of a group of PCs in a huge network by hand. Thus, we send the magic packets to the destination by providing the MAC address. The magic packet basically contains the destination computer's MAC address 255 (FF FF FF FF FF FF) that will be sent to the destination computer. The magic packet will be only checked for the MAC address and a complete protocol stack will not parse it. So, it can be sent as any network and transport-layer protocol. A link-oriented transport-layer protocol like TCP (Transmission Control Protocol) is not appropriate for this purpose because it requires a functioning connection to be formed before sending client information.

IV. NETWORK SETUP

We set up our network topology to simulate a multi-hop cross-subnet network with two arrangements of virtual PCs, each having their subnet. Furthermore, the router-to-router association is likewise viewed as its own subnet, making it a multi-hop network. Since network routing is done point to point, the number of routers does not matter, and thus we can include more hops or subnets without influencing the results. The network topology model was created utilizing GNS3 (Graphical Network Simulator-3) [5]. Table 1 shows subnet masks & IP configuration. Figure 1 shows the model network configuration.

TABLE 1. SUBNET MASK AND IP CONFIGURATION

	Router1	Router2	PC1	PC 2	PC 3	Windows server	Kali linux server
Interface0	10.1.1.1	20.1.1.1	10.0.0.6	20.0.0.7	20.0.0.8	10.1.1.118	20.1.1.50
Interface1	2.1.1.1	2.1.1.2	N/A	N/A	N/A	N/A	N/A

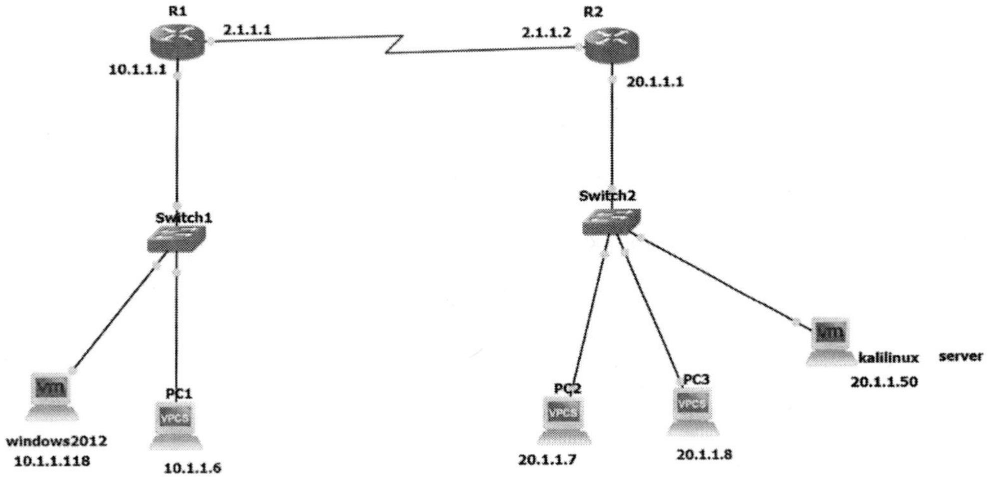

Figure 1. Model network configuration

The following procedure describes the communication from PC1 to PC2 in the WoL network in our simulation:

1. Switch1 holds the MAC address of the PC1 and Switch2 holds the MAC addresses of PC2 & PC3
2. When it pings 20.1.1.7(PC2) from PC1(10.1.1.6), the IP goes to the network gateway 10.1.1.1 which is the IP address of Router 1
3. Router 2 advertises its own network (20.1.1.2/24) and broadcasts it to other Routers
4. when Router 1 receives 20.1.1.0/24 network information, it checks for the shortest path and the advertising Routes it has.
5. Since Router 1 has the network path of the destination ones, Router 1 sends the network (20.1.1.0/24) to Router 2.
6. Router 2 receives the IP address of 20.1.1.7/24 from PC1 of Router 1 and sends it to the Switch 2 port of PC2.
7. Switch 2 receives IP address 20.1.1.7. Switch 2 holds the MAC address of PC2. Now the Switch 2 sends the received packet to the PC2 based on the MAC address.

A. *Advantage of Using WoL*

Any office files and equipment can be accessed remotely with the described WoL setup. This setup is more useful for network administrators or IT people who are working remotely, as it enables full access to a computer despite being remote. When it is combined with the correct set of remote tools, WoL technology can be used as a possible remote approximation of being in the office.

B. Disadvantage of Using WoL

There are some security concerns when utilizing this technology. First, most WoL compatible adapters do not distinguish between which PC is sending the magic bundle. This means that anyone on a network with a good and compatible IP address can possibly remotely access the computer. Thus, such a technology should be handled with additional network security provisions.

V. CONCLUSION AND FUTURE WORK

Although WoL is a generally mature technology, numerous associations and organizations do not execute it due to confinements. In this work, we implemented a simple operation management to perform important functions such as security patch delivery and framework maintenance by utilizing WoL. Given the developing nature of this technology, future research is needed to do more simulations to increase robustness because our work is still premature stage. We will also discuss with the IT department to apply our system to the live network.

ACKNOWLEDGMENT

Mr. C. R. Dendi assisted with simulations of operations.

REFERENCES

[1] M. Stefanovic, D. Przulj, M. Vukmanovic, and S. Ristic, "Mutual Impact of High Computer Network Utilization and Business Processes", International Scientific Conference on Industrial Systems, 2007.

[2] Jithin, "What is SYN Flood attack and how to prevent it?", https://www.interserver.net/tips/kb/syn-flood-attack-prevent/, 2016, [retrieved: March 2023].

[3] Sheetg09, Mestew, Aczechowski, Dougeby, "How to configure Wake on LAN in Configuration Manager", https://learn.microsoft.com/en-us/mem/configmgr/core/clients/deploy/configure-wake-on-lan, 2022, [retrieved: March 2023].

[4] CISCO, "How to configure the router to minimize a Denial of Service (DOS) attack", https://community.cisco.com/t5/security-documents/how-to-configure-the-router-to-minimize-a-denial-of-service-dos/ta-p/3117624, [retrieved: March 2023].

[5] GNS official website, "GNS-3 download" https://www.gns3.com, [retrieved: March 2023].

Model Inconsistencies and Solution Approaches to Maintain Consistency in Model-based Systems Engineering

Thomas Schumacher, David Inkermann
Institut fuer Maschinenwesen
Technische Universitaet Clausthal
38678 Clausthal-Zellerfeld, Germany
Email: {schumacher, inkermann}@imw.tu-clausthal.de

Abstract—**An effective interdisciplinary engineering process of modern systems requires linked system and domain models. This linkage results frequently in model inconsistencies, for instance conflicting information or different data types. In this paper, different types of inconsistencies, established solution approaches and challenges in Model-based Systems Engineering are derived to introduce an approach for maintaining model consistency. Therefore, a structured literature analysis is performed including 47 research papers. Based on the analysis five challenge types, ten inconsistency types and four approaches to maintain model consistency were identified. To foster model consistency this paper introduces the use of heterogeneous models. This approach combines different solution approaches to overcome crucial inconsistency and challenge types.**

Keywords-Model-based Systems Engineering; Model inconsistencies; Heterogeneuos models.

I. Introduction and Problem Description

Model-based Systems Engineering (MBSE) is a common approach to manage the complexity when developing modern system. MBSE aims at the introduction of a comprehensive system model instead of document-based approaches as a central information and communication basis [1]. A comprehensive system model integrates system requirements, behavioural and structural system definitions as well as design constraints or test results and enables the stakeholder to study the system from different viewpoints. Stakeholder, like systems engineers or mechanical engineers, viewpoints differ based on their concerns or interests on the system. Since an effective engineering requires intensive collaboration of different engineering domains and their specific viewpoints have to be integrated. However, this integration frequently causes model inconsistencies [2]. Thereby, model inconsistencies can be understood as logical contradiction or irrational existence among facts, artefacts or concepts [3]. Inconsistent models can lead to extraordinary increase of costs and development time [2] or can have serious consequences, like failed missions in aeronautics [4].

A. *Linkage of System Model and Domain Models*

MBSE including the different engineering tasks and a central system model that is typically modelled using the Systems Modeling Language (SysML), provides various benefits. Core advantages that are frequently reported are improved collaboration of different engineering domains, enhanced information consistency or increased system understanding, in comparison to traditional document-based System Engineering [5]. To achieve these advantages the use of an appropriate modelling method, modelling language and modelling tool are required [6]. In addition to this domain-independent models domain-specific models are needed, e.g., to describe the subsystems regarding geometry and spatial structure. Thereby an efficient engineering process of modern systems requires a linkage between these different model types (system and domain models), for instance by using information exchange procedures [1]. However, this information and data exchange is often facing different challenges, like incompatible data structures, since various models and tools are used and even when the information can be exchanged, the consistency of this model information still remains a challenge [7].

B. *Research Objective*

Objective of this contribution is to maintain model consistency during the development of modern systems. Therefore, a literature study was performed in order to identify challenges in MBSE based on model inconsistencies, different types of model inconsistencies and solution approaches to maintain consistency. Moreover, this contribution introduces the use of heterogeneous models within the engineering process as a combination of different solution approaches to ensure model consistency and to overcome crucial inconsistency and challenge types.

Based on the objective within this contribution the following research questions will be addressed:

- Which different types of model inconsistencies can be distinguished?
- Which different solution approaches are established in order to maintain model consistency?
- Which challenges in MBSE, and which model inconsistency types can be addressed by the application of heterogeneous models?

The paper is organized as follows: Section II explains what model inconsistencies in MBSE are and what solution approaches to maintain model consistency are available. Within Section III, the results of the study are presented, showing challenges within MBSE based on model inconsistencies, different types of model inconsistencies and solution approaches. The application of heterogeneous models and their added value to maintain model consistency will be discussed in Section IV. The paper is concluded by a summary and an outlook on further research.

II. State of the Art

The following section introduces the term model inconsistency and presents approaches to handle inconsistencies or to maintain model consistency.

A. *Model Inconsistencies within MBSE*

Inconsistencies between different models is a key challenge in MBSE [8]–[10]. Basically, inconsistency can be understood as logical contradiction or irrational existence among facts, artefacts or concepts [7][11]. In the context of this paper, we understand model inconsistency as the violation of domain-specific or domain-independent engineering rules or constraints, as stated by Vogel-Heuser et al. [7]. There are many examples for model inconsistencies, like violation of well-formedness rules, inconsistencies in redundant information, mismatches between model and test data and not following heuristics or guidelines [3][11]. Based on the high variety of inconsistencies, this paper will introduce different types of model inconsistencies that can occur within MBSE. Herzig et al. [11] investigated the fundamentals of model consistency and concluded that it is impossible to maintain model consistency during the development of complex technical systems. Therefore, in the following section different approaches for management of model inconsistencies will be presented, based on literature.

B. *Approaches for Inconsistency Management*

One of the major challenges of a classical document-based Systems Engineering is to ensure that system specification does not contain any contradicting information [11], which represents one typical kind of inconsistency. To handle this challenge MBSE introduces the idea of using a comprehensive system model, as cross-linked set of computer-interpretable models [1], to specify the system and thereby increasing the level of formalism [11]. The application of a formalized system model supports maintaining consistency in early design phases when for example the overall system architecture will be developed. With progressive development the domain-specific engineering domains are required to develop the detailed system design. Typically, domains applying domain-specific engineering approaches and models, like state-machine diagrams in the software domain or CAD-models in the mechanical domain. Accordingly, especially at the interface between system model and domain models inconsistencies can occur. To reduce the amount of model inconsistencies typically three different approaches for inconsistency management can be distinguished: proof-theory-based, rule-based and synchronization-based approaches [10][12]. Following these different approaches will be explained.

1) *Proof-theory-based approaches*

The application of a proof-theory-based approach for inconsistency management was initially proposed by Finkelstein et al. [13] for model-driven software engineering. They transform multi-view software models (e.g., class and sequence diagrams) to a first-order logic to identify inconsistencies using automated theorem prover and domain-specific rules (specified as a temporal logic) [10][12]. Core idea of this approach is the transformation of graphical representations (diagrammatic models [14]) in more formal, mathematical terms, in which inconsistencies can be identified [12].

2) *Rule-based approaches*

In a rule-based approach rules are used to describe the conditions that a model must satisfy. Thereby these conditions can used as positive or negative constraints. Satisfying positive constraints indicate that the model can be considered as consistent. Satisfying negative constraints conversely indicates model inconsistencies [12]. For this approach different applications are available in literature, like [15][16]. For mechatronic systems, Feldmann et al. [8] propose the Resource Description Framework (RDF) as a concrete representational formalism for models. By applying query languages, like SPARQL, different inconsistency types can be identified [12].

3) *Synchronization-based approaches*

The target of synchronization-based approaches is to synchronize semantically related models [12]. Therefore, model transformation is required, to provide linkage of model elements between different model types [10]. Model transformation can be distinguished into two categories: (1) use of customized modelling languages and (2) use of transformation rules [10]. Customizing modelling languages aims at an appropriate linkage of different model types. In literature SysML is often customized, by creating domain-specific profiles. An example is the profile SysML4Modelica which was created to link models based on the complementary languages SysML and Modelica [17]. The second opportunity to synchronize models is the use of transformation rules, like Triple Graph Grammars (TGGs) [18]. These rules ensure the linkage between different model elements. If a model element is changed (e.g., changed property of a model element) the change will propagate to all related model elements [12]. Overall, model transformation can ensure interoperability between different modelling languages and thereby enable domain-specific development teams to apply their known modelling languages and tools [10].

In this section, an overview about established approaches for inconsistency management was provided rely on either proof-theoretic, rule-based or model synchronization (using model transformation) approaches. To generate a more detailed understanding about different kind of inconsistencies and solution approaches within the following section different types of inconsistencies and solutions approaches will be derived and allocated.

III. Challenges in MBSE, Types of Model Inconsistencies and Solution Approaches

This section will introduce challenges in MBSE, different types of model inconsistencies and solution approaches to maintain model consistency based on an exploratory study. Figure 1 illustrates the procedure of the study. Based on a defined searching string 47 publication were identified within Scopus. The first ten publications were used to define types (categories) for challenges, inconsistencies, and solution approaches. Therefore, all mentioned challenges, inconsistencies and solutions approaches in regards to MBSE were identified and afterwards categorized into different types. The categorizing was performed by thematical and namely merging. For example, all inconsistencies regarding information or data were combined into one category or the solution type model execution contains all types of model simulation. Afterwards the remaining publications were reviewed by considering the defined categories. Finally, the review results were evaluated. We consider the amount of 47 publications for the literature study as sufficient to identify crucial MBSE challenges, inconsistency types and solution approaches. A higher number of publications will probably change the enumerations and the presented ranking, but we assume that the identified categories will still the same. Sub-sections A, B and C present the result of the literature study. In sub-section D, solution approaches will be allocated to inconsistency types.

A. *Types of Challenges in MBSE*

The first intent of the literature study was the identification of challenges within MBSE based on model inconsistencies. Figure 2 presents five challenges which are frequently reported in literature. Thereby, the challenge ***maintaining consistency*** between different models can be considered as the main challenge in MBSE. Further presented challenges are ***interoperability of modelling tools***, ***visualize specific model views***, ***management of inconsistencies*** and ***maintaining traceability***.

These challenges particularly occur due to the collaboration of multiple domains during the development of modern systems [10]. Different domains develop the system from different viewpoints because they have different interests on the system. Consequently, inconsistencies may occur in the course of the entire engineering process, like architecture definition, domain-specific implementation, integration and verification and validation. The major target is to maintain model consistency during the entire engineering process or if required to identify and solve any model inconsistencies at the time of creation in order to minimize costs and development time.

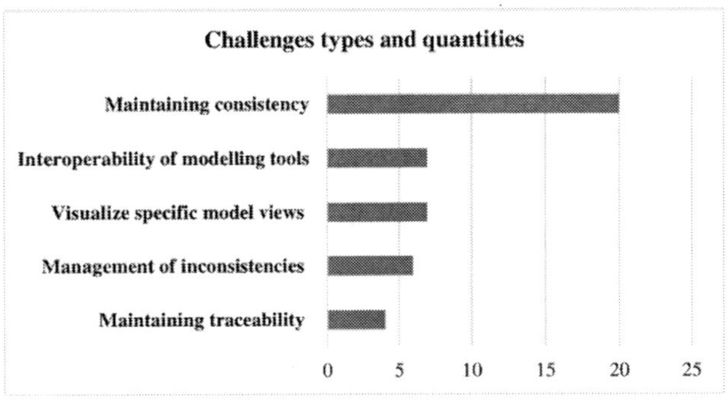

Figure 2. Identified challenge types and quantities.

The following sub-section presents different types of inconsistencies in order to avoid their creation or to locate and maintain them during the engineering process.

B. *Types of Model Inconsistencies*

Based on the performed exploratory study ten different types of model inconsistencies were identified. Figure 3 presents each type and how often they were determined during the study. By evaluating the study result, it can be concluded that six out of ten inconsistency types are more frequently stated in literature (at least five enumerations). In the following each type of inconsistency is described.

Data and information inconsistency could be determined most during the study (18 times). This inconsistency type reflects model elements with conflicting information or different data types. For instance, the system properties described in a CAD-model contradicts the initial defined properties in a system model. ***Representation inconsistency*** describes inconsistencies within the model representation. Typically, this kind of inconsistencies is caused by application of multiple models and different views and perspectives. ***Refinement inconsistency*** is typically caused by modelling of elements on different abstraction level. ***Viewpoint inconsistency*** emerges by overlapping viewpoints. The definition of viewpoints is based on various factors, like concerns of interest or responsibility.

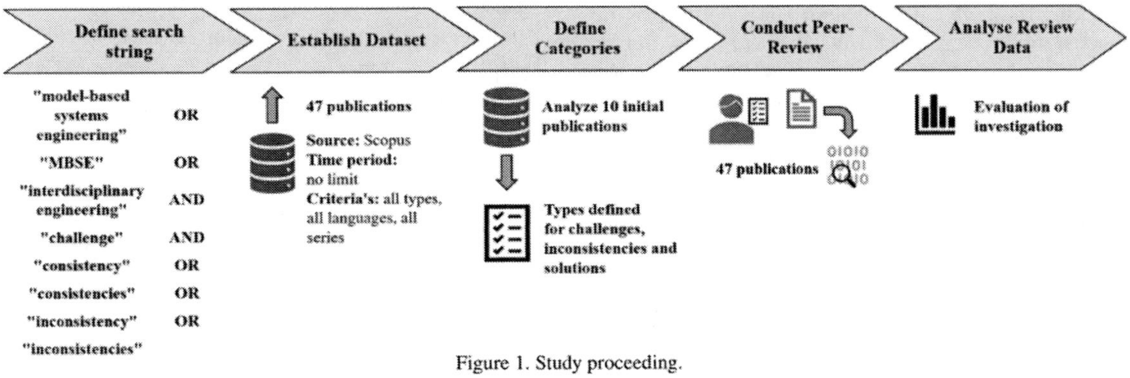

Figure 1. Study proceeding.

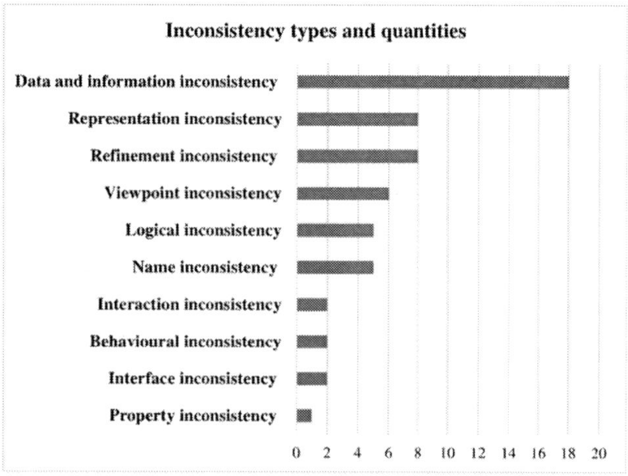

Figure 3. Identified inconsistency types and quantities.

Logical inconsistency summarizes all inconsistencies which are caused by applying different or informal modelling languages. Not following a given formal semantics and syntax can lead to logical contradictions within the model. ***Name inconsistency*** can arise when model elements have same or unconventional name, or the naming conventions are not followed. Based on literature four additional inconsistency types with sparsely amount of enumerations can be determined. ***Interaction inconsistency*** describes the execution of model operations which violates interaction constraints, like the order of model operations. ***Behavioural inconsistency*** contains an unexpected behaviour of model elements. ***Interface inconsistency*** arises when model elements describing interfaces have conflicting values, terminologies, or schemas. ***Property inconsistency*** occurs when model elements contradict constraints regarding element properties or values.

C. *Types of Solution Approaches*

The papers out of the study were also analysed regarding approaches to handle model consistencies. These solutions can be classified into four overall categories: ***model execution***, ***tool interoperability and data exchange***, ***model abstraction*** and ***model formalization***. Thereby *model execution* and *tool interoperability and data exchange* are the most frequently reported approaches, see Figure 4.

Model execution contains all approaches regarding actively checking for model inconsistency by model simulation, for instance a model element expects an energy flow but has only material or informational relations, or the use of inconsistency pattern. For safety relevant systems model assessments applying simulation-based fault injection approaches to identify failures in the system design and behaviour are established. Moreover, all approaches explained in Section II.B are included in this category. ***Interoperability of modelling tools*** are focusing on establishing standardized interface specifications, like Open Services for Lifecycle Collaboration (QSLC) or Functional Mock-up Interface (FMI). Also, part of this solution type are all approaches considering *data exchange* among modelling tools. Therefore, many contributions propose the application of universal data formats and schemas, like Automation Markup Language (AML) or Standard for the Exchange of Product Data (STEP). A further approach is the use of meta-models and ontologies to link model elements on a more abstract level. These are classified into the solution type ***model abstraction***. The use of (semi)formal modelling language is an additional approach to reduce model inconsistencies, this goes along with a higher ***model formalization*** and reuse of knowledge, like model pattern. These two types were distinguished because a model formalization does not always go along with an abstraction and vice versa. The following sub-section will allocate these solution approaches to the identified inconsistency types.

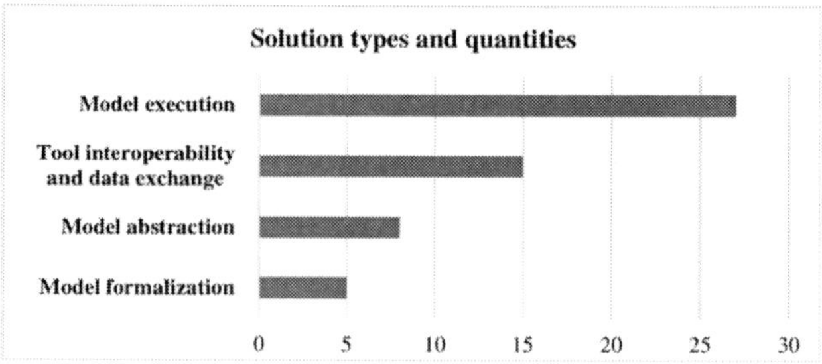

Figure 4. Identified solution types and quantities.

D. *Allocation of Solution Approaches to Inconsistency Types*

To achieve the overall objective to maintain model consistency it is important to locate and solve the different model inconsistencies. Therefore, Table I contains an allocation between the identified inconsistency types and solution types.

TABLE I. ALLOCATION OF SOLUTION AND INCONSISTENCY TYPES

Inconsistency type	Solution type
Data and information inconsistency	Model execution
	Tool interoperability and data exchange
Representation inconsistency	Model execution
Refinement inconsistency	Model abstraction
Viewpoint inconsistency	Tool interoperability and data exchange
Logical inconsistency	Model formalization
Name inconsistency	Model execution
	Tool interoperability and data exchange
Interaction inconsistency	Model execution
Behavioural inconsistency	Model execution
Interface inconsistency	Model execution
	Tool interoperability and data exchange
Property inconsistency	Model execution
	Tool interoperability and data exchange

This allocation gives advice which solution types can support managing the different inconsistency types.

In general, it can be conducted that caused by the high variety of model inconsistencies a consistent model-based engineering process requires different solution approaches in parallel to ensure model consistency.

Therefore, we introduce the application of heterogeneous models as an approach combining different solution approaches to maintain model consistency.

IV. APPLICATION OF HETEROGENEOUS MODELS TO MAINTAIN MODEL CONSISTENCY

The establishment of heterogeneous models in MBSE supports by overcoming the following identified challenges: ***maintain consistency***, ***interoperability of modelling tools***, ***visualize specific model view*** and ***maintaining traceability***. Thereby following inconsistency types will be addressed: ***data and information inconsistency*** due to the linkage of model elements based on data structure. ***Representation inconsistency*** due to the integration of different views and perspectives into one model and ***refinement*** and ***logical inconsistencies*** due to the integration of model elements with different abstraction or different semantics and syntax into one presentation. This is made possible due to the combination of following solution types: ***model synchronization*** as part of model execution, ***tool interoperability and data exchange***, ***model abstraction*** as well ***model formalization***.

Following the application of heterogeneous models will be explained by visualization of heterogeneous models and presentation of a technical interface concept to link different model types. Thereby, we are focusing on model consistency between SysML and CAD-models, which represent domain-independent and domain-specific models.

Heterogeneous models offer the possibility to integrate different sub-models or model elements into one model presentation [19]. As an example, Jansen presents a mechatronic leg as a heterogeneous model, which integrates three-dimensional objects, two-dimensional substitute models including their relations and additional information about the context of the system, like assembly space restrictions [20]. Thus, heterogeneous models can be applied to integrate model elements with different abstraction and formalization level, like SysML-elements as domain- independent models and CAD-elements as domain-specific models, into one model [21]. Figure 5 presents a mock-up of a heterogeneous model, which combines CAD- and stereotyped SysML model elements. This model can support for example by system architecture definition, due to the integration of behaviour descriptions (yellow oval) and their allocation to the physical system structure and the combination of interface descriptions based on SysML-elements (ports and interface blocks) and their relations to the physical system elements.

Premise for consistent heterogeneous models are linked model elements. Therefore, the data structure of each model element needs to be investigated and linked. Figure 6 presents a concept for linking SysML- and CAD model elements based on the universal data types XML and STEP [22].

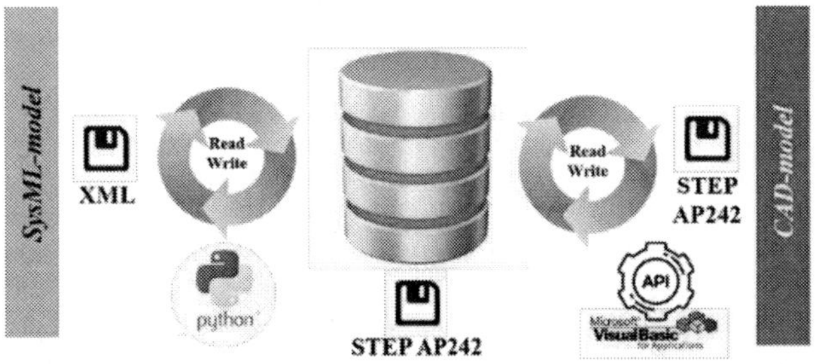

Figure 6. Technical interface concept [22].

Key elements of these interface are two applications for data transfer. First a Python-based application which interprets the data between XML and STEP files and second a VBA-based application programming interface (API), which controls the data in- and output into the CAD-tool. More details about the technical interface and their application can be seen in [22].

It can be conducted that the application of heterogeneous models can be a great support by maintaining model consistency due to the combination of different solution approaches. Thereby, the number of model inconsistencies based on different inconsistency types can be reduced.

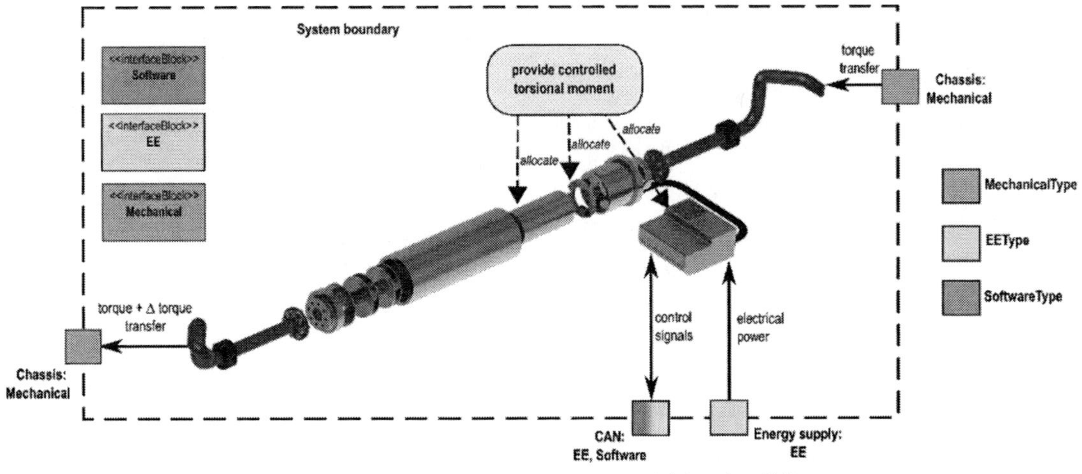

Figure 5. Visualization of a heterogeneous model, based on [21].

V. Conclusion

This paper depicts the need of linked system and domain models in interdisciplinary engineering. This linkage is often a common cause for model inconsistencies. Therefore, within this paper different challenges in MBSE, types of model inconsistencies and established solution approaches to maintain model consistency were determined. Based on a performed literature study, ten different inconsistency types, four solution types and five challenges were identified. Following the solution types were allocated to inconsistency types to locate and solve potential model inconsistencies. Furthermore, this contribution introduces heterogeneous models as an approach for maintaining model consistency. Heterogeneous models based on a linked data structure combine different solution types to maintain model consistency and offer the opportunity to create meaningful models for specific engineering activities. With these models, the occurrence of different inconsistency types can be prevented and thus substantial challenges within MBSE supported. Future research is focusing on the evolution and application of heterogeneous models based on a linked data structure. Therefore, different modelling tools will be investigated to integrate CAD- and SysML-model elements into one model.

Acknowledgment

Funded by the Lower Saxony Ministry of Science and Culture under grant number ZN3493 within the Lower Saxony "Vorab" of the Volkswagen Foundation and supported by the Center for Digital Innovations (ZDIN).

References

[1] S. Friedenthal, A. Moore, and R. Steiner, A practical guide to SysML: The systems modeling language (The MK/OMG Press). Waltham, MA: Elsevier/Morgan Kaufmann, 2015.

[2] G. Spanoudakis and A. Zisman, "Inconsistency Management in Software Engineering: Survey and Open Research Issues," in Handbook of Software Engineering and Knowledge Engineering, 2001, pp. 329–380.

[3] S. J. I. Herzig and C. J. J. Paredis, "A conceptual basis for inconsistency management in model-based systems engineering," Procedia CIRP, vol. 21, pp. 52–57, 2014, doi: 10.1016/j.procir.2014.03.192.

[4] B. Nuseibeh, "Ariane 5: Who Dunnit?," IEEE Softw., vol. 14, no. 3, pp. 15–16, 1997, doi: 10.1109/MS.1997.589224.

[5] K. Henderson and A. Salado, "Value and benefits of model-based systems engineering (MBSE): Evidence from the literature," Systems Engineering, vol. 24, no. 1, pp. 51–66, 2021, doi: 10.1002/sys.21566.

[6] L. Delligatti, SysML distilled: A brief guide to the systems modeling language. Upper Saddle River, NJ: Addison-Wesley, 2014.

[7] B. Vogel-Heuser et al., "Challenges of interdisciplinary development of Cyber-Physical Production Systems," At-Automatisierungstechnik, vol. 67, no. 6, pp. 445–454, 2019, doi: 10.1515/auto-2018-0144.

[8] S. Feldmann et al., "Towards effective management of inconsistencies in model-based engineering of automated production systems," IFAC-PapersOnLine, vol. 28, no. 3, pp. 916–923, 2015, doi: 10.1016/j.ifacol.2015.06.200.

[9] A. M. Madni and M. Sievers, "Model-based systems engineering: Motivation, current status, and research opportunities," Systems Engineering, vol. 21, no. 3, pp. 172–190, 2018, doi: 10.1002/sys.21438.

[10] A. Berriche, F. Mhenni, A. Mlika, and J.-Y. Choley, "Towards model synchronization for consistency management of mechatronic systems," Applied Sciences (Switzerland), vol. 10, no. 10, pp. 1–20, 2020, doi: 10.3390/app10103577.

[11] S. J. I. Herzig, A. Qamar, A. Reichwein, and C. J. J. Paredis, "A conceptual framework for consistency management in model-based systems engineering," Proceedings of the ASME Design Engineering Technical Conference, vol. 2, pp. 1329–1339, 2011, doi: 10.1115/DETC2011-47924.

[12] S. Feldmann et al., "A comparison of inconsistency management approaches using a mechatronic manufacturing system design case study," in 2015 IEEE International Conference on Automation Science and Engineering (CASE), Gothenburg, Sweden, 2015, pp. 158–165, doi: 10.1109/CoASE.2015.7294055.

[13] A. Finkelstein, G. Gabbay, A. Hunter, J. Kramer, and B. Nuseibeh, "Inconsistency Handling in Multi-Perspective Specifications," in 1993 -Proceedings of the 4th European Software Engineering Conference, pp. 84–99.

[14] "Diagrammatic Models," in Intuition in Science and Mathematics (Mathematics Education Library), Dordrecht: Kluwer Academic Publishers, 2002, pp. 154–166.

[15] T. Mens, R. van der Straeten, and M. D'Hondt, "Detecting and Resolving Model Inconsistencies Using Transformation Dependency Analysis," in Model Driven Engineering Languages and Systems (Lecture Notes in Computer Science), D. Hutchison et al., Eds., Berlin, Heidelberg: Springer Berlin Heidelberg, 2006, pp. 200–214.

[16] A. Egyed, "Automatically Detecting and Tracking Inconsistencies in Software Design Models," IIEEE Trans. Software Eng., vol. 37, no. 2, pp. 188–204, 2011, doi: 10.1109/TSE.2010.38.

[17] C. J. Paredis et al., "An Overview of the SysML-Modelica Transformation Specification," INCOSE International Symposium, vol. 20, no. 1, pp. 709–722, 2010, doi: 10.1002/j.2334-5837.2010.tb01099.x.

[18] F. Klar, A. Königs, and A. Schürr, "Model Transformation in the Large," in Proceedings of the 6th joint meeting of the European software engineering conference, Dubrovnik Croatia, I. Crnkovic and A. Bertolino, Eds., 2007, pp. 285–294, doi: 10.1145/1287624.1287664.

[19] S. Jansen and E. G. Welp, "A Heterogeneous Modelling Approach for Domain Allocation in Mechatronics," Guidelines for a Decision Support Method Adapted to NPD Processes, 2007.

[20] S. Jansen, A methodology for model-based partitioning of mechatronic systems. Aachen: Shaker, 2007.

[21] T. Schumacher and D. Inkermann, "Heterogeneous models to Support Interdisciplinary Engineering - Mapping Model Elements of SysML and CAD," Procedia CIRP, vol. 109, pp. 653–658, 2022, doi: 10.1016/j.procir.2022.05.309.

[22] T. Schumacher, D. Kaczmarek, D. Inkermann, and A. Lohrengel, "Fostering Model Consistency in Interdisciplinary Engineering by Linking SysML and CAD-Models," in 2022 IEEE International Symposium on Systems Engineering (ISSE), Vienna, Austria, 2022, pp. 1–7, doi: 10.1109/ISSE54508.2022.10005327.

Modeling of a Railroad Worker Protection System Architecture in PFS

Lucas T. Macedo, Fabrício Junqueira, Paulo E. Miyagi
Universidade de São Paulo, Escola Politécnica
São Paulo, Brazil
e-mail: {macteslucas, fabri, pemiyagi}@usp.br

***Abstract*—The metro system is an important transportation mode for urban cities. This system has had a long operation time since its construction, is still operating, and will not be replaced easily. Hence, it can be classified as a legacy system. Moreover, the metro system requires preventive or corrective maintenance, because there are still situations and occurrences that cannot be properly predicted. During the corrective maintenance, the metro line is still running while the railroad worker is also on the railway. In this situation, the operator, from the Operations Control Center (OCC), must create a safe area for the railroad worker to carry out the maintenance. Although the metro line has safety procedures, training, and rules for this situation, a miscommunication or leak of the operator's attention might make the railroad worker vulnerable to accidents. Based on that, this paper focuses on providing an architecture in which the railroad worker is considered protected automatically. The railroad worker protection system architecture is modeled using the Production Flow Schema (PFS), as well as the metro one, to present the architectures` operation and the interaction between the two architectures.**

Keywords: metro system; legacy system; protection system architecture; production flow schema.

I. INTRODUCTION

The metro system is a transportation mode characterized by being capable of transporting people or goods, at high velocity and with a high level of safety [1]. In a big city, such as São Paulo (Brazil) for instance, approximately 81 million people used metro lines 1, 2, and 3 in January 2020. Beyond that, the metro system is the most efficient option to be implemented in urban areas based on the space occupied compared to the other types of transportation [1].

Another characteristic of the metro system is the long operating time. In some cases, the metro system in London (England) has been working since 1890, in Chicago (USA) since 1897 [2], and in São Paulo (Brazil) since 1974 [3]. Considering this operating time and the old technology used on these systems, they can be regarded as legacy systems. Legacy systems are running systems that do not comply with the emerging architectural standards but still meet some functional business needs [4]. Moreover, legacy systems cannot be easily stopped because of the critical information in their operational code and database. Lastly, legacy systems demand frequent and complex maintenance [5].

The metro system comprises different equipment responsible for controlling energy consumption, passenger flow, managing rail devices, and supporting operating the line. Equipment or devices in general need maintenance, mainly when they have a long operating time, such as the ones that belong to the metro system. When maintenance of railway equipment is required during metro line operation, such as a broken rail, for example, some safety actions are required to allow local safe maintenance while the remaining line continues to run. The operator, who is monitoring and controlling the line, takes these actions manually. If these actions are not taken properly, the railroad worker, carrying out the field maintenance, is unsafe.

According to the company responsible for managing the metro lines in São Paulo, there were 57 accidents between 2017 and 2021 on the railway in São Paulo. These accidents are related to inadequate management of the tools, same-level fall, not following the internal procedure, and bumping on objects or equipment. Although none of the accidents reported by the company were fatal, fatal ones were found in the São Paulo metro history.

A 30-year experienced railroad worker was run over by a metro car. He was wearing Personal Protection Equipment (PPE). The accident's cause was the lack of communication between the operator and the railroad worker [6]. In another case, the railroad worker was electrocuted, while he was executing maintenance on a circuit breaker that was badly signalized. In addition, the railroad worker reported communication issues between him and the operator. Although the railroad worker was wearing PPE, he was aware of the safety rules, and had years of experience, these were not enough to protect him [7].

Some similar cases were found outside Brazil. In New York (USA), for instance, a railroad worker was taken to a hospital with severe injuries [8]. According to the news, he had five years of experience and there were lights and signals to avoid accidents. However, this was not enough to stop the train on time. In London (England), an inspector was run over by the train during his work routines [9]. In this case, there was a system to alert the inspector about the train arriving, but this was also not enough to protect him. It was described by the local news that this system was only able to alert the inspector, not to take action to guarantee the inspector's protection.

The common reason for these accidents is the miscommunication between the railroad worker, who is executing the maintenance on the field, and the operator, who is the Operations Control Center (OCC) monitoring not only the maintenance activities, but the whole metro line. This issue is also highlighted in [10] as the main reason that keeps the railway insecure in London. Hence, a system focused on automatically protecting the railroad workers during their activities shall create a new layer of protection for them and avoid miscommunication-related accidents, such as touching an energized power rail, being hit by a train or energized switch rail, and not being quickly notified about a fire detection on the railway.

Although a new system needs to be added to the metro architecture, the metro system is a legacy system, and as such, cannot be changed easily. Hence, the new system architecture shall run separately of the metro architecture. Furthermore, the interface points between the two architectures shall be mapped to reduce the changes needed in the metro architecture. In summary, the contribution of this paper is the presentation of a railroad worker protection architecture that protects the railroad worker and can communicate with the metro architecture with minimum interference. Beyond that, this paper shows a railroad worker protection system architecture and metro system architecture modeled using the Production Flow Schema (PFS).

The remainder of this paper is divided into five sections. Section II presents the projects and papers related to worker protection in railway/metro systems. Section III describes the metro system architecture. Section IV focuses on PFS. After this, Section V models the metro and railroad worker protection system architecture in PFS. Finally, Section VI is the conclusion.

II. Related Work

The section lists projects/papers that highlight solutions to improve the railroad worker safety during his tasks on field.

The authors of [11] propose a system to detect if the rail vehicle is next to the railroad worker location. This system uses fiber optic interferometers as vibration sensors to detect the rail vehicle next to him. Once a rail vehicle is detected, the authors suggest optical or acoustical signal to alert the railroad worker.

The authors of [12] present a wearable Global Navigation Satellite System (GNSS) sensor to track the railroad worker in rail worksites. His position is used to verify if the railroad worker is in any dangerous area. Although this paper focuses on protecting the railroad worker, it does not clarify how to protect him, only how to detect if he is in a dangerous area.

The Litum company developed a safety system that monitors in real-time the construction workers during the construction of the Paris subway expansion [13]. This project used Ultra-Wideband Radio-Frequency Identification (UWB RFID) attached to the 400 construction workers' helmets. Beyond that, the tunnel where the construction workers were is 33km long in total and they received alarms by e-mail through Wi-Fi. The goal of this system was to ensure that only authorized construction workers were in the restricted areas, the number of construction workers in specific areas were not exceeded, confirmed that all workers followed the directions, and the system was capable to react quickly in potential cases of emergency.

The author of [14] suggests a safety mechanism that uses image analyses to verify whether a track segment is damaged or not. The author focuses on the SkyTran track, but this solution can be applied to other rail tracks. Although this solution can prevent derailing, and consequently damage to the railroad worker, this paper does not present how this system will be integrated to any railway system.

Lastly, the authors of [15] propose a solution in which the railroad worker is alerted when the train arrival time to his position is 30 seconds or less. In this solution, the railroad worker wears wearable device that contains a Global Position System (GPS) sensor, radio receptor device and actuators to create tactile, visual, and sound alerts. Moreover, a GPS sensor and radio transmitter, signaling on broadcasting mode, are attached to the train.

Although the solutions presented in this section focus on the railroad worker safety, gathering more data from him and keeping him updated, most of them require that he or any other operator react to guarantee the railroad worker safety. The goal of this paper is beyond that; it is to monitor and protect the railroad worker automatically, not depending on anyone's reaction, once activated.

III. Metro System

The São Paulo's metro system can be divided into two main systems: Signaling and Control System (SCS) and Central Control System (CCS). The SCS is responsible for rail equipment management, metro position and protection, and passenger safety on the metro. The CCS is responsible for station management, equipment monitoring and control, and passenger safety in the station. These systems interchange information, such as train position, fire detection, power consumption, etc. These systems can be seen in Figure 1.

According to [16], the SCS follows the IEEE 1474.1-2004 [17], which described the requirements to execute the Communications-Based Train Control (CBTC). In other words, it describes the system requirement to allow the train to run safely and automatically. The SCS is divided into three subsystems: Automatic Train Protection (ATP), which certifies that the train has a speed-maximal threshold for the metro car in each section of the railway to ensure a safe road, protecting the train from collisions; Automatic Train Operation (ATO), that shall define the metro road, metro velocity (following the maximum speed established by

ATP), and the waiting time in each station; and Automatic Train Supervision (ATS), that is the SCS supervisory, presenting the position and status of the metro and rail devices on operator's screen. The ATP and the ATO are usually defined by regions. Hence, they are presented as Regional ATP (RATP) and Regional ATO (RATO).

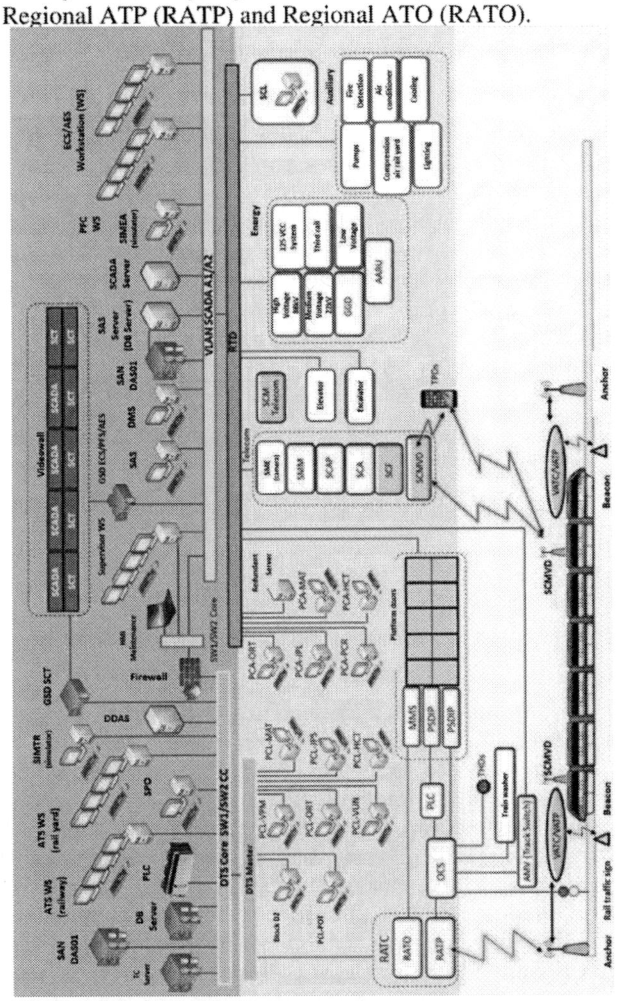

Figure 1. São Paulo's metro system architecture translated into English [18].

The CCS has a central Supervisory Control and Data Acquisition (SCADA) component that monitors and controls the equipment in the metro line. The CCS is also divided into three subsystems: Electric Control System (ECS), Passengers Flow Control system (PFC), and Auxiliary Equipment System (AES). For instance, the ECS monitors and controls electric devices, such as feeders, third rail, and circuit breakers. Beyond that, the ECS monitor the demand and power consumption. The PFC controls the passenger flow. Therefore, this subsystem monitors and controls cameras, elevators, escalators, etc. Finally, all other devices, such as fire detectors, cooling devices, pumps, tanks, networks, and multimedia devices are included in the AES.

The metro system has an OCC where the workstations, SCADA server, ATS server, videowall, and others are located. From the OCC, the operator can monitor and control the metro line. Furthermore, the operator can communicate remotely with the railroad worker through Walkie-Talkie.

It is important to highlight that, besides the metro system being a legacy system, the metro architecture also follows the automation pyramid proposed by International Society of Automation (ISA) in ISA-95 [19], as can be seen in Figure 1. This means the three bottom layers of ISA-95 (field, control, supervisory) are present in this architecture, from bottom to top: field layer is indicated in yellow; control layer is shown in green; and supervisory layer in red. Lasty, due to a huge number of devices present in each system, this paper will focus on two of them from each system:

- **CCS:** we present the behavior of the feeder, a circuit breaker used in middle voltage to feed the power rail, because the power rail is not directly controllable, and the fire detector. The feeder status is opened or closed, and can be commanded to open or close. The fire detector status is activated or not activated. Note that there is no command for the fire detector;
- **SCS:** we present the behavior of the rail switch and the metro car. The rail switch status is like the CCS equipment. In other words, the device status is energized or de-energized, and can be commanded to energize and de-energize. Whereas the train can be understood in a different way, the train behavior is based on the speed thresholds in a specific area. The ATP defines this and can be controlled by the ATS. If the speed threshold is 0, the area is blocked for the train. If it is not 0, the train can pass through that area.

IV. PRODUCTION FLOW SCHEMA

Production Flow Schema (PFS) is an interpreted graph from Petri Net (PN) to model Discrete Events Systems (DES) in an abstract level [20]. The PFS was designed to systematize and facilitate the modeling process, because system modeling processes are done in a natural language, and the mathematical formalism is guaranteed due to the net structure.

The PFS allows abstract model improvement using a top-down approach exploring the macro events [21]. Furthermore, this graph does not have a token, different from the PN, because the PFS focuses on the structural description of the items flow and system data. However, when reaching the appropriate level of detail for the study, a PN or Colored Petri Net (CPN) model can be directly generated to carry out analysis through simulation.

The PFS is also considered a bipartite graph compound of activity elements (action, execution), distributing elements (collect, accumulate and/or store items), and oriented arcs to connect the elements [22]. These elements and the different structures allowed in PFS can be seen in Figure 2.

It is important to highlight that the communication flow between different modules can only be used, if the data/item used in each net is different and if this arc represents the data flow between the activity elements.

According to [23], EN 50128, which defines software development requirements for railway applications, highly recommend the use of semi-formal methods (like PN, and consequently PFS and CPN) for developing safety related software for railway application to satisfy the safety requirements. In addition, [24] presents the advantage of the PN comparing it to other safety analysis tools, such as expanded Failure Mode & Effects Analysis (FMEA), and Hazard and Operability (HAZOP). Based on that, PN, PFS and CPN are applicable for safety applications. Lasty, there are several applications of the PN and CPN in railway applications, for instance [25] and [26], but they do not focus on protecting the railroad worker.

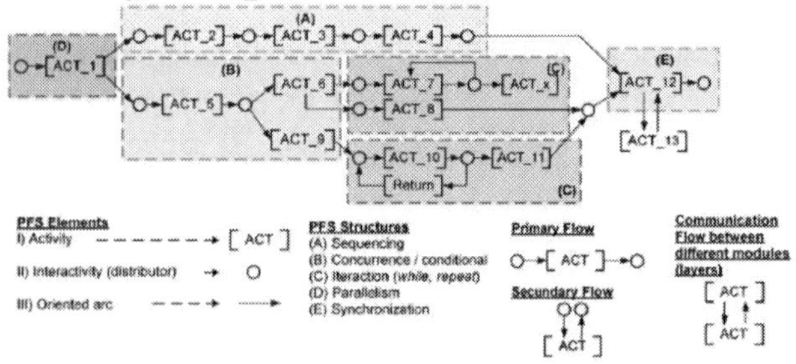

Figure 2. Elements, structures and flows in PFS [21].

The conversion from the PFS to the PN was used in [20], and can be explain through an example in Figure 3. In this picture, the PFS model can be seen in the left side, and the equivalent of this PN model in the right side. Note that the activities can be replaced by one or more places in the PN model, and the brackets by transitions. If there is an arc entering or leaving the activity in the middle, a transition shall be added. Moreover, the communication flow between different modules is represented by a transition fusion in the PN, as can be seen by the transition **{t1}**. The mark position should be decided at the end of the modeling process.

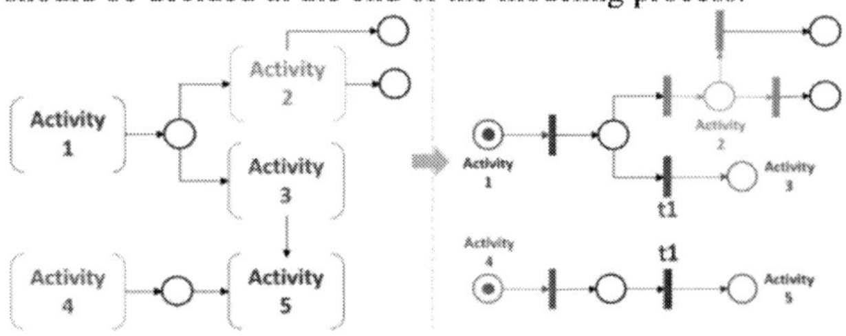

Figure 3. Example of conversion from PFS to PN.

Since the PFS focuses on the architecture structure, the model of the metro system architecture, more specifically São Paulo's one, and railroad worker protection system architecture in the PFS are presented in the next sections. Thus, the architecture structure, through the architecture models and interaction between each other, must be defined, before executing simulation analysis. If the architecture structure is wrong, it will be useless, even though the results of the simulations are positives. Moreover, this paper will present only PFS due to space available.

V. ARCHITECTURES MODELING

The railroad worker protection architecture shall follow the same division in three macro activities, and color, as shown in Figure 4. The goal is a system that works automatically. Hence, it needs to acquire railroad worker positions in real-time to know which equipment and area shall be interlocked. Beyond that, it needs a real-time channel to inform the railroad worker of alarms. These two requirements are related to **[Railroad Worker Protection Field]**.

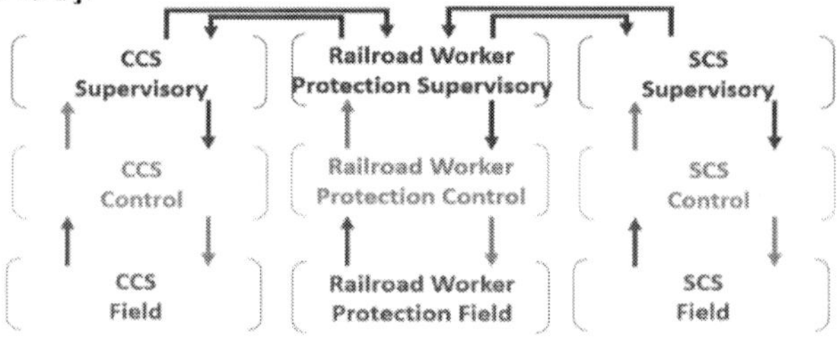

Figure 4. Main activities of the metro and rail worker protection system architecture.

[Railroad Worker Protection Control] shall start and stop the railroad worker position request if there is any on the railway. Moreover, this layer shall also prepare a database of pre-recorded voice message to be sent to railroad workers based on the alarm message.

Finally, **[Railroad Worker Protection Supervisory]** shall monitor and manage the protection of the railroad worker. Moreover, it shall interface with the other systems.

Since all equipment data in a metro architecture are in **[CCS Supervisory]** and **[SCS Supervisory]**, this system architecture will interface with the existing metro architecture through the supervisory layer. In addition, the equipment commands shall be executed initially by **[CCS Supervisory]** and **[SCS Supervisory]**. Finally, **[Railroad Worker Protection Supervisory]** shall be responsible for identifying the equipment to be interlocked in each system.

Although CCS and SCS supervisory are interchanging information as reported in Section III, this information does not affect the railroad worker protection system architecture. Hence, this connection is not presented in PFS model.

A. *Metro System Architecture*

[CCS Supervisory] and **[SCS Supervisory]** can be modeled as represented in Figure 5 and Figure 6. First, they receive equipment status from the control activity **{1} {5}**. The equipment status can be transferred to other systems **{A} {C}**. From the CCS or SCS to other systems, such as the railroad worker protection system. Subsequently, data from the other systems is received **{B} {D},** and then, the equipment command to the control activity can be sent. For instance, when the equipment command to interlock from the railroad worker system architecture is received, the command shall be sent to the control layer in this step **{2}{6}**. Finally, restart the loop.

[CCS Control] and **[SCS Control]** have two main tasks: (1) Receive the command from the supervisory **{2} {6}** and deliver to the field equipment **{3} {7}**; (2) Receive the equipment data from the field **{4} {8}** and deliver to the supervisory **{1}{5}**.

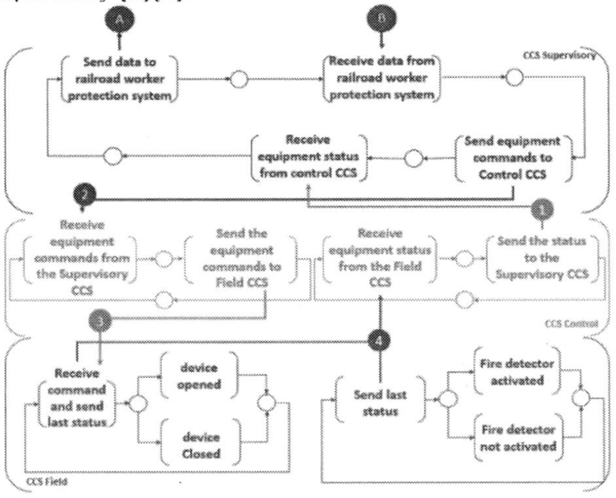

Figure 5. CCS architecture modeled in PFS. "A" and "B" continues in Figure 7.

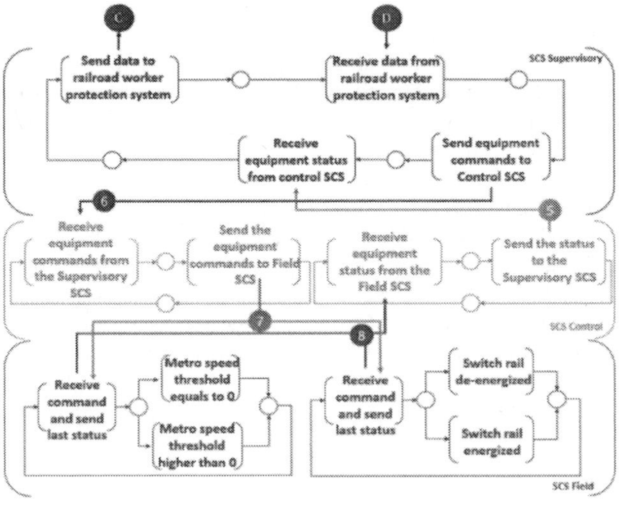

Figure 6. SCS architecture modeled in PFS. "C" and "D" continues in Figure 7.

[CCS Field] and **[SCS Field]** have the same structure, but equipment used in each model are different. Therefore, to each loop, the last equipment data acquired is sent to the control layer **{4} {8}**, and the command, received from control activity **{3} {7}**, is executed. If the equipment does not have command, this layer shall only send the equipment status. Finally, as discussed in Section III, the behavior of the Feeder and fire detector is highlighted and modeled for the CCS Field. The behavior of the rail switch and the metro car is highlighted and modeled for the SCS Field.

B. Railroad Worker Protection Architecture

The railroad worker protection architecture requires tracking the railroad worker in real-time, and according to [15] can be used a wearable device for this task, represented in **[Railroad Worker Protection Field]**. Beyond that, the railroad worker can be updated automatically through audio messages on Walkie-Talkie **[Messages received via Walkie-Talkie]**, such as fire alarm messages. In this case, the railroad worker can also manage his safety once he is well-informed.

[Railroad worker Protection Control] shall acquire the railroad worker position **[Railroad worker data request]**. This data shall be shared to **[Calculate railroad worker protection area]**. In addition, this layer prepares the message to be sent via Walkie Talkie **[Send audio messages to railroad worker]**.

On **[Railroad worker Protection Supervisory]**, there are six main requirements that this macro activity shall accomplish:

1) **[Calculate railroad worker protection area]:** calculates based on the railroad worker position and position lost alarm;

2) **[Recognize the equipment to be interlocked]:** compares the railroad worker position with the equipment status, and train location to select the equipment that shall be interlocked to guarantee the railroad worker safety. This information is sent to the **[Middleware]** to forward to metro system;

3) **[Show on screen the railroad worker data]:** indicates on screen the railroad worker position and his status in real-time;

4) **[Alarm management to keep railroad worker updated]:** gathers alarms from the **[Middleware]**, for example fire detection to update the railway worker;

5) **[Middleware]:** allows the communication between the metro and railroad worker system. This activity shall send the device list and commands to the metro system, gather the device status from there and filter the status that are alarmed;

6) **[Railroad worker registration management]:** the operator shall insert the railroad worker in the system, to trigger the logics, and remove it, in case the maintenance is over.

Each activity listed above can be detailed in Figure 7 and each activity will be explained hereinafter.

The operator, knowing the necessary maintenance, shall insert the railroad worker into the system through **[Railroad worker registration management] {1}**. This triggers the other activities to run **{15}**. The activities shall continue until the operator removes the railroad worker from the system **{2}**.

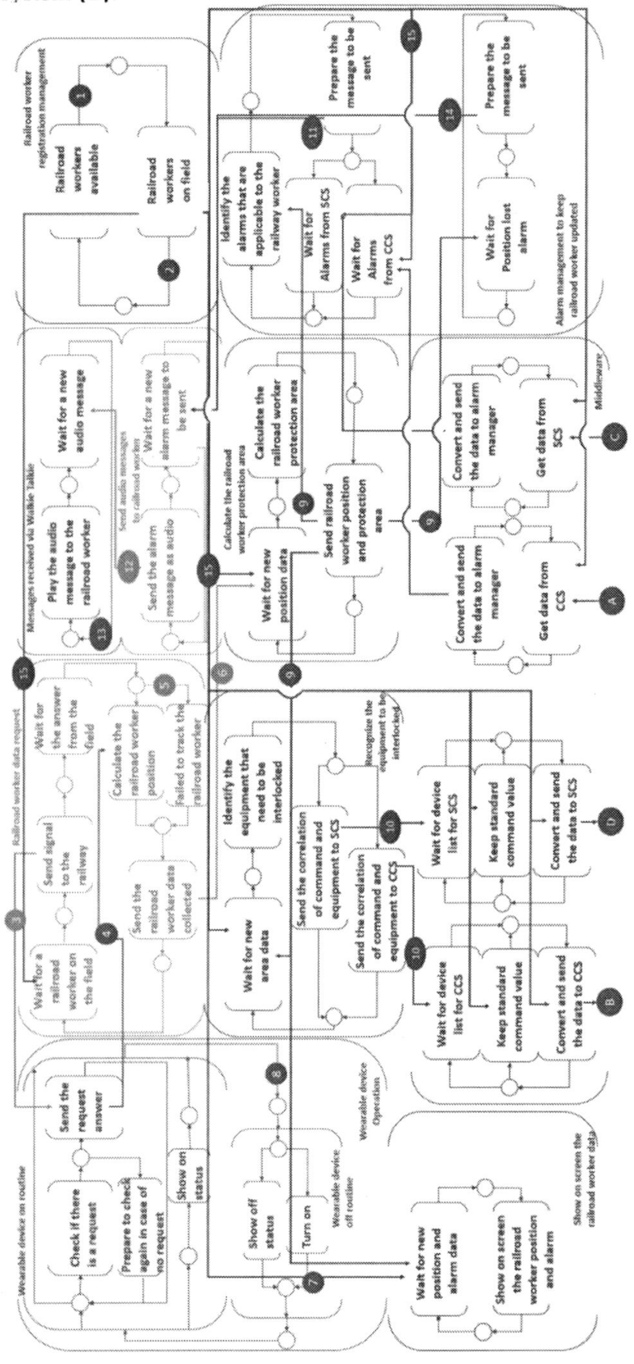

Figure 7. Refined railroad worker protection architecture modeled in PFS. "A", "B", "C" and "D" continues in Figure 5 and Figure 6.

After receiving the data that the railroad worker is on the railway, **[Railroad worker data request]** starts looking for him. First, the signals are sent to the railway, looking for the railroad worker **{3}**. If he is found, his position is calculated **{4}**. If he is not found, a flag is set to alarm the operator **{5}**. This data will be used to calculate his protection area in **[Calculate railroad worker protection area] {6}**.

The **[Wearable Device Operation]** starts off **{7}**. The railroad worker shall turn on the wearable device to be found. In case of success, the wearable device is on and ready to be found. Once a request signal for data is received **{3}**, the reply signal is sent back **{4}**. The wearable device keeps in this loop until the railroad worker turned the wearable device off **{8}**.

The railroad worker position and position lost alarm are used to calculate a protection area around him in **[Calculate railroad worker protection area] {6}**. The area value are variation of x and y position called delta X and delta Y. In case of position lost, the railway worker protection area results in a bigger area than the last calculation to protect him, if he is nearby. After calculating the delta X and Y, these values with the railroad worker position (x and y values) are sent to other activities **{9}**.

[Recognize the equipment to be interlocked] uses the protection area **{9}** to match the devices position and identify the devices in that area. After that, the list of the SCS and CSS equipment that shall be interlocked is sent to **[Middleware] {10}**.

[Alarm management to keep railroad worker updated] uses the protection area **{9}** to match the alarms activated on SCS and CSS **{11}**. Once the alarms that apply to the railroad worker area are recognized, the messages are converted to the voice message in **[Send audio messages to railroad worker] {12}** and then sent to railroad workers via Walkie Talkie in **[Message received via Walkie-Talkie] {13}**. In addition, the railroad worker shall be also informed through Walkie-Talkie in case of losing his position **{14}**.

[Show on screen the railroad worker data] uses the position and area of the railroad worker to show his position on the screen. The screens are maps of the railway with alarm banner. Therefore, the operator can see the railroad worker position, his protection area, and any alarm related to him, such as loss of his position.

Lasty, the railroad worker protection system architecture must interface with metro one, considering it as a legacy system, through **[Middleware]**. Therefore, the devices and command devices shall be sent to metro system in a way that it can process this information **{B} {D}**. Furthermore, this architecture shall be capable of collecting device data to inform him properly **{A} {C}**.

VI. CONCLUSION

The metro system has been demonstrated to be essential to urban cities, mainly because of its capability of transporting, occupying less space in comparison to other transport modes. This legacy system, compounded of many devices, requires repair. Once a maintenance is needed, the railroad workers are sent to the railway to fix the issue. The accident reports during maintenance have shown that current safety actions are insufficient to protect the railway worker. Hence, a railroad worker protection system architecture is needed to protect him automatically.

It was concluded that the interface between the metro and railroad protection system architecture shall be done through the supervisory layer, because metro's SCADA gathers the metro line data. The metro system architecture shall command the equipment to an interlock status. The PFS can be used to generate the model of the railroad worker protection system architecture.

Finally, the contribution of this paper is the presentation and modeling of an architecture that focuses on protecting the railroad workers automatically since activated, taking in consideration that metro system is legacy system, in other words, reducing changes on the metro system; and on simplifying the supervision procedures in OCC. Although it was applied the architecture to São Paulo's metro system, this architecture shall be applicable for any metro system. It has only to understand the system that the railroad worker protection system architecture is being applied to and where this architecture can communicate with the metro one. Furthermore, its construction in PFS allow the uses of formal method as PFS to convert into PN [20] or CPN, and subsequently into programming languages [27].

A. *Further work*

The PFS model presented will be used to generate the CPN model of the railroad worker protection system architecture, metro system architecture and their interaction. Finally, the CPN model will be simulated to verify and validate the proposed architecture. It will be verify if all states reachable are safe and there is no deadlock or live lock in the modeled system, as done in [25] and [26].

REFERENCES

[1] D. Lin, W. Broere, and J. Cui, "Metro systems and urban development: Impacts and implications," Tunn. Undergr. Sp. Technol., vol. 125, no. March, p. 104509, 2022, doi: 10.1016/j.tust.2022.104509.

[2] M. Dugdale, "World's oldest metro systems - Railway Technology," May 28, 2019. https://www.railway-technology.com/analysis/worlds-oldest-metro-systems/ (accessed Apr., 2023).

[3] M. Oliveira, "11 curiosities about SP Metro," Sep. 17, 2021. https://mobilidade.estadao.com.br/mobilidade-para-que/dia-a-dia/11-curiosidades-sobre-o-metro-de-sp/ (accessed Apr, 2023).

[4] H. K. M. A. Bakar, R. Razali, and D. I. Jambari, "Implementation phases in modernisation of legacy systems," Int. Conf. Res. Innov. Inf. Syst. ICRIIS, vol. December-2, 2019, doi: 10.1109/ICRIIS48246.2019.9073628.

[5] S. M. Hussain, S. N. Bhatti, and M. F. U. Rasool, "Legacy system and ways of its evolution," Int. Conf. Commun. Technol. ComTech 2017, pp. 56–59, 2017, doi: 10.1109/COMTECH.2017.8065750.

[6] G1 SP, "Technicians killed by train in SP did not comply with the norm, says Metro".Dec, 2011. https://g1.globo.com/sao-paulo/noticia/2011/12/tecnicos-mortos-por-trem-em-sp-descumpriram-norma-diz-cptm.html (accessed Apr 01, 2023).

[7] Terra, "Metro is condemned in case of work accident with electrician," Jan. 28, 2020. https://www.terra.com.br/noticias/dino/metro-e-condenado-em-caso-de-acidente-de-trabalho-com-eletricista,8d78dc7d1d57c51f431b71cf33e23f65h8ujnte1.html (accessed Apr, 2023).

[8] D. Meyer and T. Moore, "Subway worker's foot severed, leg 'shattered' by oncoming Q train," 2022. https://nypost.com/2022/01/10/nyc-subway-worker-hospitalized-after-being-struck-by-train/ (accessed Apr, 2023).

[9] S. Della Sala, "Investigation underway after Amersham track worker struck by London Underground train," Jul. 25, 2022. https://www.buckinghamshirelive.com/news/buckinghamshire-news/investigation-underway-after-amersham-track-7369351 (accessed Apr, 2023).

[10] T. Farrington-Darby, L. Pickup, and J. R. Wilson, "Safety culture in railway maintenance," Saf. Sci., vol. 43, no. 1, pp. 39–60, 2005, doi: 10.1016/j.ssci.2004.09.003.

[11] S. Kepak et al., "Fibre optic portable rail vehicle detector," 20th Slovak-Czech-Polish Opt. Conf. Wave Quantum Asp. Contemp. Opt., vol. 10142, no. December 2016, p. 101421M, 2016, doi: 10.1117/12.2257061.

[12] M. D'Arco, A. Renga, A. Ceccarelli, F. Brancati, and A. Bondavalli, "Enhancing workers safety in worksites through augmented GNSS sensors," Meas. J. Int. Meas. Confed., vol. 117, no. December 2017, pp. 144–152, 2018, doi: 10.1016/j.measurement.2017.12.005.

[13] Litum, "Construction Worker Tracking and Safety: Paris Metro | Litum," Oct. 08, 2019. https://litum.com/blog/worker-tracking-rtls-construction-paris-metro/ (accessed Apr, 2023).

[14] Y. Wiseman, "Safety Mechanism for SkyTran Tracks," *Int. J. Control Autom.*, vol. 10, no. 7, pp. 51–60, 2017, doi: 10.14257/ijca.2017.10.7.05.

[15] B. V. Ferreira et al., "Wearable computing for railway environments: proposal and evaluation of a safety solution," IET Intell. Transp. Syst., vol. 11, no. 6, pp. 319–325, 2017, doi: 10.1049/iet-its.2016.0187.

[16] P. Lima and R. Santos, "Signaling and Control System of Line 15," São Paulo, 2013. https://www.aeamesp.org.br/biblioteca/stm/19smtf130913T41rl2.pdf. (access Apr, 2023).

[17] R. Transit, V. Interface, and S. Committee, "IEEE standards," IEEE Acoust. Speech, Signal Process. Newsl., vol. 37, no. 1, pp. 5–6, 2012, doi: 10.1109/msp.1976.237495.

[18] São Paulo's department of metropolitan transport, "Design of railway systems for line 15," 2017. http://www.parcerias.sp.gov.br/Parcerias/Documento/Download?codigo=26535 (accessed Apr., 2023).

[19] ISO standard, "ISO/IEC 62264-1:2013 Enterprise-control system integration Part1: Models and terminology," 2013.

[20] M. A. Pisching, M. A. O. Pessoa, F. Junqueira, and P. E. Miyagi, "PFS/PN Technique to Model Industry 4.0 Systems Based on RAMI 4.0," IEEE Int. Conf. Emerg. Technol. Fact. Autom. ETFA, vol. 2018-Septe, pp. 1153–1156, 2018, doi: 10.1109/ETFA.2018.8502573.

[21] M. A. Pisching, M. A. O. Pessoa, F. Junqueira, D. J. dos Santos Filho, and P. E. Miyagi, "An architecture based on RAMI 4.0 to discover equipment to process operations required by products," Comput. Ind. Eng., vol. 125, no. January, pp. 574–591, 2018, doi: 10.1016/j.cie.2017.12.029.

[22] D. Filho, F. Nakamoto, F. Junqueira, and P. Miyagi, "Task control of intelligent transportation vehicles in manufacturing systems," in Mechatronics Series I - Intelligent Transportation Vehicles, BENTHAM SCIENCE PUBLISHERS, 2012, pp. 146–169.

[23] U. Yildirim, M. S. Durmus, and M. T. Soylemez, "Application of Functional Safety on Railways Part I: Modelling & Design," ASCC 2011 - 8th Asian Control Conf. - Final Progr. Proc., pp. 1090–1095, 2011.

[24] D. Vernez, D. Buchs, and G. Pierrehumbert, "Perspectives in the use of coloured Petri nets for risk analysis and accident modelling," Saf. Sci., vol. 41, no. 5, pp. 445–463, 2003, doi: 10.1016/S0925-7535(01)00078-9.

[25] H. Song, J. Liu and E. Schnieder, "Validation, verification and evaluation of a Train to Train Distance Measurement System by means of Colored Petri Nets," Reliab. Eng. Syst. Saf., vol. 164, no. March 2016, pp. 10–23, 2017, doi: 10.1016/j.ress.2017.03.001.

[26] P. Sun, S. Collart-Dutilleul, and P. Bon, "A model pattern of railway interlocking system by Petri nets," 2015 Int. Conf. Model. Technol.

Intell. Transp. Syst. MT-ITS 2015, no. June, pp. 442–449, 2015, doi: 10.1109/MTITS.2015.7223292.

[27] A. Mello, M. Barbosa, D. Filho, P. Miyagi and F. Junqueira, "A Transcription Tool From Petri Net To Clp Programming Languages," ABCM Symp. Ser. Mechatronics, vol. 5, pp. 781–790, 2012.

Software Engineering Project Management with the Community of Practice Approach: Toward Changes in Software Engineering Education

Charlie Y. Shim
Dept. of Comp. Sci. & Info. Tech.
Kutztown University of Pennsylvania
Kutztown, PA, USA
e-mail: shim@kutztown.edu

Yeungkwun Kim
School of Computer Science
Western Illinois University
Macomb, IL, USA
e-mail: Y-Kim2@wiu.edu

Injoo Kim
Dept. of Comp. & Info. Sci.
East-West University
Chicago, IL, USA
e-mail: injoo@eastwest.edu

Abstract—**In this paper, we propose to integrate the Community of Practice (CoP) approach into software engineering classroom environment and develop CoP sessions for software engineering courses. Incorporation of the CoP method rejuvenates the importance of human and social aspects and trains students to be equipped with teamwork skills essential for establishing a mutually supportive and collective learning working environment, such as software development.**

Keywords – Software Engineering; Community of Practice; Human and Social Aspects; Collective Learning; Classroom Environment.

I. INTRODUCTION

Software engineering has frequently been used as a capstone course for many computer science programs in academia. The importance of people-related issues and teamwork skills in software engineering have been recognized and resulted in many researches [1]-[4]. Recent trends in information technology project management, such as globalization, outsourcing, and virtual teams [5] have even been boosting the role of human and social factors. Based on these, it is obvious that students should start to practice teamwork skills that could handle people-related issues and launch working environments for mutually supportive and collaborative learning from their school years.

Students, however, often criticize the classroom environment where instructors discuss people-related issues in an extremely limited way so that students cannot receive enough assistance or instruction on how to work effectively in a team [6]. We also found similar results from informal interviews with students. For the question, "What was the most challenging issue that you faced while working on a capstone project in software engineering course?" students frequently answered they had a hard time in "managing efficient communication among team members", "addressing conflicts among team members", and "adjusting unfair contribution among team members", which all need teamwork skills based on human and social aspects.

It seems that the students' real problem does not exist in applying software engineering knowledge to a capstone project, but does exist in handling people-related issues properly. Instructors may put this down to many challenges in a classroom environment, such as limits in time and opportunities, differences in students' background, etc. As we saw in current trends, human and social factors are no longer an option that can be postponed. Students should experience and learn how they effectively work as a team in the classroom environment and be ready to establish mutually supportive and collective learning working environment in the real world. In the swim of this, we should consider integrating a systematic process of teaching and evaluating teamwork skills based on human and social factors as a part of a software engineering course.

The CoP is a group formed by people who regularly engage in sharing and learning, based on their common interests [7]. Many organizations integrated the CoP method as a part of their organization structure with the purpose of improving their performance [8]. Adopting this method into the classroom environment will provide students with chances to build teamwork skills to manage people-related issues needed for software engineering project management. In this research, we propose to adopt the CoP method and develop CoP sessions that are specific to a software engineering course, where we believe is the right place to incorporate this approach.

The rest of this paper is arranged as follows. Section II describes the related concepts of software engineering, human aspects in software engineering, CoP, and key elements of CoP. Section III describes the commonalities between CoP and software engineering project management. CoP sessions designed for a software engineering course and issues to consider are also discussed. The conclusion and future study end the paper.

II. RELATED WORK

A. *Software Engineering and Human Aspects*

The Institute of Electrical and Electronics Engineers (IEEE) defines Software Engineering as "the application of a systematic, disciplined, quantifiable approach to the development, operation, and maintenance of software" [9]. It is common for many computer science programs to assign two consecutive semesters for a software engineering course. Students learn software engineering skills and knowledge during the first semester, then apply the skills and knowledge to complete a capstone project of software development during the second semester. Since software engineering is where students can simulate real-world working environments through a project, it has frequently been developed as a project-based capstone course in many computer science programs. Human and social factors play as much an important role as academic knowledge in a project-based course like software engineering. Students who successfully complete the course are expected to have the ability to understand user needs, work within a team framework, and participate in the overall process of the project management.

B. Community of Practice

The CoP is an educational literature that refers to a network of peers who share a common interest in a particular topic and come together to fulfill both individual and group goals [10]-[11]. Through such networks, members wish to collaborate with other members by sharing information and developing knowledge [10]. The community of practice consists of three key elements [10]:

- **Mutual Engagement** – Individual understanding should be supported by a practical and meaningful connection among members obtained by real contribution of members to complement each other.
- **A Joint Enterprise** – The community should have a context of being part of a broader system and operated through a process of collective negotiation.
- **A Shared Repertoire** – The community should standardize terms used in discussions.

We believe the CoP approach in the educational technology field can be considered as a possible solution to integrate a systematic process of teaching and evaluating human and social factors as a part of a software engineering course.

III. Integrating The Community of Practice Approach into Software Engineering Course

A. Understanding Software Engineering Project Management in the Context of Community of Practice

Three key elements of the CoP mentioned in Section II.B are also essential for the area of software engineering, especially for software engineering project management:

- **Mutual Engagement** – A successful project management mandates individual member's clear understanding of the project. This can be accommodated by active communication among team members. The environment of mutually supportive and collaborative learning through active communication can promote a truly cohesive relationship among members and their strong contribution to the project.
- **A Joint Enterprise** – A systems approach is popularly adopted for a successful project management. In this approach, top management and project managers should understand how projects are related to the whole organization. A project should be considered within the larger organizational context and operated in a wide organizational environment.
- **A Shared Repertoire** – Team members' clear understanding of a project is essential for a successful project management. To help their understanding, use of standardized terminology and maintaining efficient communication channels among members are necessary. Records of communication history and definitions of standardized terminologies can be included as a part of the project management document.

B. Designing Community of Practice Sessions for Software Engineering Class

As we discussed in Section III.A, the CoP approach and software engineering project management share similarities in their main goals. Given the similarities, we propose to adopt the CoP approach for the software engineering course. Table 1 shows the outline of the CoP sessions that we designed for a software engineering course.

We assumed a two-semester structure mentioned in II.A. Thus, the activities in Table 1 can be implemented during the second semester while students work on a capstone project using the knowledge obtained from the first semester. For one semester software engineering course, some of the sessions can be combined and the weeks to do the activities can be adjusted to fit into the class schedule. Table 1 lists only CoP activities that will be integrated into an existing software engineering class schedule.

C. Issues to Consider

The core of the commonalities between CoP and software engineering project management exists in the issues of people and their cohesive interactions. The following issues should be considered when integrating CoP for project management into the software engineering classroom:

- **Size and Members** – Each project team formed in a software engineering classroom will work as a CoP. Based on our teaching experience, we propose to form a team of 3 to 5 members. The appropriate size for a team can be properly adjusted according to a classroom environment. The bigger the size, the harder to maintain close cohesion among members. Team members with various backgrounds in their coursework and other experiences may be helpful for accommodating a collaborative learning environment among members.
- **Communication** – Efficient communications among team members are crucial for the success of

TABLE 1. OUTLINE OF COP SESSIONS FOR A SOFTWARE ENGINEERING COURSE

#	Week	Activity Description
S1	1	***CoP Concept*** - The instructor introduces the idea and importance of the CoP. - The instructor explains how and where the CoP will be integrated into software engineering project management - The instructor checks students' understanding of the CoP
S2	1	***Review of Teamwork Principles*** - The instructor reviews teamwork principles and their importance. - The instructor introduces the common problems that teams from previous semesters had.
S3	2	***Project Concept*** - Team members have a general discussion about the nature of the project. - Each member should represent their understanding of the project and get feedback from other members. - Through the discussion, members help each other to understand the project and make sure they are on the same page.
S4	2	***Scope of Assigned Work*** - Each team member clearly understands their role in the project and clear scope of the assigned job.
S5	3	***Communication and Evaluation Method*** - Team members adopt a standard method of communication among the members. - Team members adopt an evaluation method for each member's contribution.
S6	8	***Intermediate Evaluation for the CoP activities so far*** - Team members discuss whether communication among members has been maintained effectively so far. - Team members discuss whether mutually supportive and collective learning environments have been maintained so far. - Team members discuss other project management related issues. - Team members plan on necessary changes for the identified issues. - The instructor performs intermediate surveys on students' teamwork experience.
S7	15	***Final Evaluation*** - Team members have a final discussion on their teamwork experience with the project management. - Team members evaluate other members contribution to the project. - The instructor performs final surveys on students' teamwork experience.

the CoP and the project. Meetings are the most common way of managing communication among members. Keeping meeting minutes is recommended to address possible confusion and misunderstanding. The use of social network services, such as a blog, can also be considered. Creating and maintaining a CoP blog for the project management could be helpful for a team with meeting schedule issues. Instead of face-to-face meetings, members could maintain communication through the blog.

- **Effectiveness** – Measuring the effectiveness of the applied CoP sessions will make the approach more robust and meaningful. In Table 1, two forms of surveys (i.e., intermediate, and final) were proposed for this. Comparisons between the two survey results are expected to demonstrate how students' experience has been improved. Details on the contents of the proposed surveys will not be discussed in this paper. That will be a part of the continued research.

IV. CONCLUSION

Despite their importance, teamwork skills needed for a project management are currently not practiced enough in the software engineering classroom. To address the issue, we proposed the adoption of the CoP method into the software engineering classroom. We justified the applicability of the CoP method to software engineering classroom environment and developed specific CoP sessions for a software engineering course. With the help of the CoP, students will understand the importance of human and social factors in a project management. Students are also expected to practice people-related issues in a systematic way and be equipped with necessary teamwork skills to accommodate mutually supportive and collective learning environment for software development.

V. FUTURE STUDY

In our future work, we will develop two surveys for the proposed CoP sessions and apply the sessions to the software engineering course. Students' experience will be assessed through the surveys. We will also discuss a possibility of designing and adopting a formal measure to assess the effectiveness of the CoP sessions integrated into a classroom environment.

REFERENCES

[1] K. Garg and V. Varma, "People Issues Relating to Software Engineering Education and Training in India," Proceedings of the ACM-SIGSOFT's 1st India software engineering conference (ISEC '08), pp. 121-128, February 2008.

[2] J. Karn and T. Cowling, "A Follow up Study of the Effect of Personality on the Performance of Software Engineering Teams," Proceedings of the 2006 ACM/IEEE international symposium on Empirical software engineering (ISESE'06), pp. 232-241, September 2006, Rio de Janeiro, Brazil.

[3] M. John, F. Maurer, and B. Tessem, "Human and Social Factors of Software Engineering: Workshop Summary," ACM SIGSOFT Software Engineering Notes, vol. 30, issue 4, pp. 1-6, July 2005.

[4] J. M. Hogan and R. Thomas, "Developing the Software Engineering Team," Proceedings of the 7th Australasian Conference on Computing Education, vol. 42, pp. 203 - 210, 2005.

[5] K. Schwalbe, Information Technology Project Management (6th Edition), Course Technology, CENGAGE Learning, 2010, ISBN: 978-0-324-78692-7.

[6] H. Su, S. Jodis, and H. Zhang, "Providing an integrated software development environment for undergraduate software engineering courses," Journal of Computing Sciences in Colleges, vol. 23, issue 2, pp. 143-149, December, 2007.

[7] E. L. Lesser and J. Storck, "Communities of practice and organizational performance," IBM Systems Journal, vol. 40, no. 4, pp. 831-841, 2001.

[8] R. McDermott and D. Archibald, "Harnessing Your Staff's Informal Networks," Harvard Business Review Magazine, March 2010. [Online] Available from: http://hbr.org/2010/03/harnessing-your-staffs-informal-networks/ar/1/ 2023.03.09

[9] IEEE Standards Collection: Software Engineering, the Institute of Electrical and Electronics Engineers (IEEE) Standard 610, IEEE, 1993.

[10] E. Wenger, Communities of Practice: Learning, meaning and identity, Cambridge University Press, 1998.

[11] E. Wenger, R. McDermott, and W. Snyder, Cultivating Communities of Practice: A Guide to Managing Knowledge, Harvard Business School Press, 2002.

Decentralized Cooperative Intersection Management Based on Connected Autonomous Vehicles for Urban Unsignalized Intersections

Jie Zhang
Ostfalia University of Appplied Sceiences
Department of Mechanical Engineering
Institute for Mechatronics
Wolfenbüttel, Germany
e-mail: jie.zhang@ostfalia.de

Marian Göllner
Ostfalia University of Appplied Sceiences
Department of Mechanical Engineering
Institute for Mechatronics
Wolfenbüttel, Germany
e-mail: mar.goellner@ostfalia.de

Xiaobo Liu-Henke
Ostfalia University of Appplied Sceiences
Department of Mechanical Engineering
Institute for Mechatronics
Wolfenbüttel, Germany
e-mail: x.liu-henke@ostfalia.de

***Abstract*— Considering the increasing population and vehicle demand, the development of a safer and more efficient intersection management system is of critical importance. The following paper addresses decentralized intersection management through synergetic cooperation of networked autonomous vehicles to optimize intersection throughput as well as ensure proactive safety of all vehicles. Through Vehicle-to-Vehicle (V2V) communication, autonomous vehicles can obtain real-time information from all road users within the effective communication range, including position, speed, direction of travel, and destination. Based on the information, the priority for crossing the intersection or the order of passage can be determined by coordination between vehicles, so that the conflict zone of the intersection always remains free of traffic. At the same time, low-priority vehicles can also adjust their speed in advance to avoid potential conflicts with other vehicles. A pilot application is used to validate and demonstrate the model-based developed intersection management in a virtual simulation environment. Quantitative analysis of the simulation results proves the performance of the management system, especially in extremely high traffic intensity where the management system can keep traffic flowing in the conflict zone, ensuring efficient operation. The generalizability of the developed management system is also verified by applying it to a complex traffic network consisting of multiple intersections.**

Keywords- Optimal intersection management; cooperative intersection control; connected autonomous vehicles; Vehicle-to-Vehicle (V2V) communication; Model-in-the-Loop-Simulations; model-based systems engineering.

I. INTRODUCTION

As urbanization continues, especially in developing countries, the demand for vehicles to satisfy travel needs is steadily increasing, while the lack and inadequacy of transportation infrastructure exacerbates the serious shortage of transportation resources and the resulting high number of traffic accidents, especially at the intersection and junctions on major roads as frequent accident blackspots in the urban road network.

Although road intersections represent a relatively small part of the total road network, they are responsible for a significant proportion of traffic accidents. According to the Community Database of the European Union (EU database: "CARE") on road accidents, more than 20% of traffic fatalities are attributable to road traffic at intersections [1]. A similar ratio is observed in the United States, where 40% of accidents and 21.5% of traffic fatalities occur at intersections [2] [3]. According to statistics from the Insurers Accident Research, in Germany in 2020, about two-thirds of all cyclist accidents with personal injury recorded by the police in urban areas occurred at intersections, junctions and driveways, with about one in five of these accidents occurring while turning right [4]. The complex traffic network and redundant traffic signals due to numerous junctions often lead to long traffic congestion on major traffic sections during peak traffic hours, which is especially common in large cities with high population density and in small and medium-sized cities with inadequate road infrastructure and is an almost universal problem for the whole society.

To efficiently address the aforementioned road traffic challenges, this paper focuses on the development of decentralized cooperative intersection management through synergetic networking of autonomous vehicles using V2V communication to optimize traffic throughput and also ensure proactive safety at the intersection. The rest of this paper is organized as follows. Section II introduces the related work and the methodology. Section III details the design of the intersection management system. In Section IV, based on representative application scenarios, the developed intersection management is validated and demonstrated in a virtual simulation environment. Section V gives the conclusion.

II. STATE OF THE ART

In this section, the state of knowledge on the topics of intersection management is first presented. Subsequently, the mechatronic development methodology for the systematic structuring of a Cyber-Physical system (CPS) is described.

A. Intersection management

Numerous scientific researches on different aspects have been carried out to optimize the traffic flow at the intersection, whose main objectives are efficiency, safety, ecology and passenger comfort, as shown in Fig. 1.

The research activities focus on the topological characteristics of the traffic system and its traffic signal control, including the design of traffic infrastructure and the geometric design of road networks, the development of more rational traffic control and speed limits, the research of more advanced traffic monitoring and enforcement techniques, and the more accurate evaluation and disposition of traffic resources through more realistic simulation of traffic systems [7] [8]. Although the developed solution approaches in focus on traffic structure can improve the traffic flow to a certain extent, the waiting time at intersections is unfortunately not eliminated regardless of the traffic intensity and thus no longer meets the increasing mobility and social demands [7]. For example, in a signal-controlled intersection, vehicles are instructed the passing order by the cycle change of red and green light, and therefore adjust their speed with the light system. This traffic control approach causes more vehicles to congest at the intersection, and the delay time for vehicles in the conflict zone increases exponentially with traffic volume [9]. That is, vehicles take more time at the intersection, causing inefficient intersection traffic, especially if road users are not evenly distributed within it. Restrictions on mobility can cause driver frustration, irritation, and stress, which encourages more aggressive driving behavior and can further slow the process of restoring a free flow of traffic. [10]

In contrast, cooperative intersection management offers a more proactive solution for scenarios without traffic signals to overcome the aforementioned challenges. cooperative intersection management is developed based on networked autonomous driving and aims at creating and executing a (global) optimal sequence for road users when crossing the intersection. Through the use of communication technology, such as Dedicated Short Range Communication (DSRC) and Celluar Vehicle-to-Everything (C-V2X), as well as their

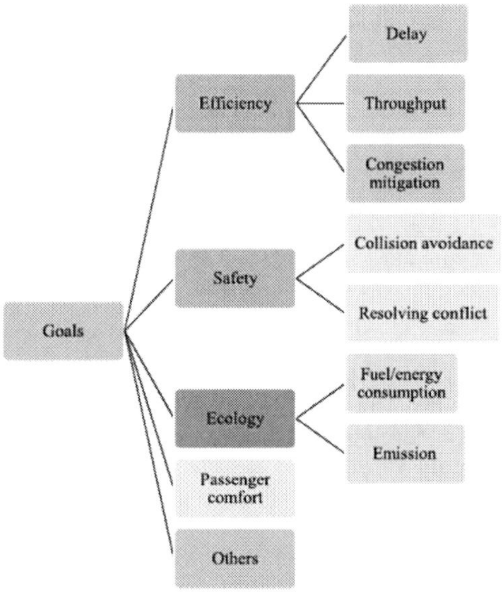

Figure 1. Research goals of intesection management [5][6].

application in autonomous vehicles and also in traffic infrastructure, effective networking with other road users is enabled, leading to early response to potential conflicts between road users in the conflict area and optimization of throughput at intersections due to the increased driving speed [5][6]. According to National Highway Traffic Safety Administration (NHSTA), the effective application of V2V and V2I communication could reduce and/or avoid up to 80% of accidents of any type without impairment [2]. Therefore, cooperative driving is an important driving strategy for future autonomous driving at intersections. In this regard, autonomous driving combines both categories of traffic safety in terms of the traffic environment and vehicles, and the cooperative driving function increases efficiency in this regard [11].

Depending on the degree of automation of road users and its structure, cooperative intersection management is divided into centralized and decentralized strategies.

In centralized approaches, it has a central Intersection Coordination Unit (ICU) that is placed in a certain area around the intersection [12] and globally decides the order or priority of passage at the intersection for all vehicles within the communication range. In [13]-[15], the methods for priority setting are presented, which are developed according to different principles, such as rule-based methods, search-based methods, optimization-based methods, and so on. The strategy mainly relies on Vehicle-to-Infrastructure (V2I) technology to achieve bidirectional communication between vehicles and road infrastructures. With access to extensive information of road users, a global optimum is delivered by ICU [5].

In contrast to centralized intersection management, decentralized intersection management eliminates the need of ICU for dispatching vehicles at the intersection by synergistically networking autonomous vehicles. The networked autonomous vehicles can recognize the current traffic situation and make decisions independently with the support of the exchanged traffic information without the help of an external decision system to fulfil transportation orders safely and efficiently [16]. In decentralized intersection management, vehicles use V2V communication to coordinate right-of-way and adjust their own trajectories. Unlike centralized intersection management, decentralized intersection management usually achieves a suboptimal solution because each vehicle only obtains local information of vehicles in a limited number [17]. In [18], an interactive decision model based on fuzzy logic with integration of conflict identification model is developed based on game theory for vehicles. In [19], a driving strategy based on cooperative game theory is presented for leading time avoidance of the conflicts between vehicles at the intersection. In [20], an algorithm for cooperative driving based on Model Predictive Control is designed for connected autonomous vehicles at unsignalized intersections. However, such approaches do not consider the impact of traffic volume on the reliability of the function.

From the perspective of the functional coverage, most recent researches pay more attention to the cooperative driving strategy of the isolated single intersection, which is called area-wide cooperative intersection management, e.g., [21]-[23]. In fact, the vehicles pass through several intersections in the road network one after another and the vehicle's behaviours at the single intersection are interdependent, which leads to the complicated interactions between vehicles. Moreover, it enables the causality loops in the trajectory planning of the vehicles, in which the calculated trajectories affect each other in different conflict zones, resulting in no reasonable solution and high calculation effort when each vehicle focusses on its optimal trajectory [24]. It should be extended to a network-wide cooperative intersection management system that deals with a road network consisting of multiple intersections. Moreover, many algorithms for isolated intersections, which are developed under certain constraints and for specific application scenarios, cannot be directly adopted for complex road networks consisting of multiple intersections.

The decentralized intersection management system based on networked fully automated vehicles developed in this paper, in contrast to the related research work mentioned above, is mainly used to solve the problem of spatial and temporal causal loops when vehicles pass through multiple intersections in succession. That is, the approach can be applied to both single intersections and road networks formed by multiple intersections, without requiring much work to be invested. The generalizability of the method is not affected by the topological characteristics of the intersection within a certain traffic flow range.

B. *Mechatronic structuring*

The domain diversity and thus the heterogeneous character of the CPS results in a high system complexity [25]. To handle the complexity of highly integrated systems in a systematic, seamless manner, a clear system and functional structure is first required.

The structuring is carried out by applying the generalized cascade principle, which provides for the use of subordinate functional modules with high dynamics by superimposed functional modules for the local implementation of global target variables [26]. Modularization and hierarchization take central place for structuring. In modularization, subfunctions are derived from the entire system in a top-down process and encapsulated in modules. In hierarchization, these functional modules are arranged hierarchically with defined interfaces. Based on a clear structuring of the entire system, a clear representation of the information flow is achieved.

The definition of the necessary function modules and the hierarchical arrangement of these is carried out using the following six structural elements [27]:

- **Mechatronic Function Module (MFM):** The MFMs are the basic elements of the system and represents the lowest level of the hierarchy. They consist of sensors, actors, information processing and basic system related mechanical structure. This functionally encapsulated modules are the most vital element of the system. It has defined physical and signal interfaces to the superordinate MFG.
- **Mechatronic Function Group (MFG):** The coupling of several MFMs results in a MFG with its own information processing and sensors. They use the subordinate MFMs with their actuators and mechanical structure. MFMs are mainly used for structuring the information processing.
- **Autonomous Mechatronic System (AMS):** Several MFGs, which are coupled by physical and signal interfaces form an AMS in their entirety An AMS is completely independent of its environment and has its own sensors and information processing. It includes the top level of the mechanical structure.
- **Cross-linked Mechatronic System (CMS):** The CMS is a signal-based coupling of several AMS and is the top hierarchical level. It coordinates and optimizes operations by regulating the flow of information and passing on decisions that affect all the AMSs in the network.
- **Autonomous Function Group (AFG):** If several AMS are networked with each other so that they can exchange information. A swarm is formed, which is called AFG. The autonomy of each individual AMS is still given, only the sum of available information has grown. The AFG has additional sensors that provide data for all subordinate AMS. The difference to the original definition of the CMS is, that no decisions are made for subordinated systems, but information is exchanged, and cooperative operation is possible.
- **Cross-linked Function Group (CFG):** Several CMSs can be grouped across domain boundaries as CFG, so that data can be exchanged in structured clusters. A CFG establishes an exchange of information between the CMS in the sense of a complete networking and digitalization.

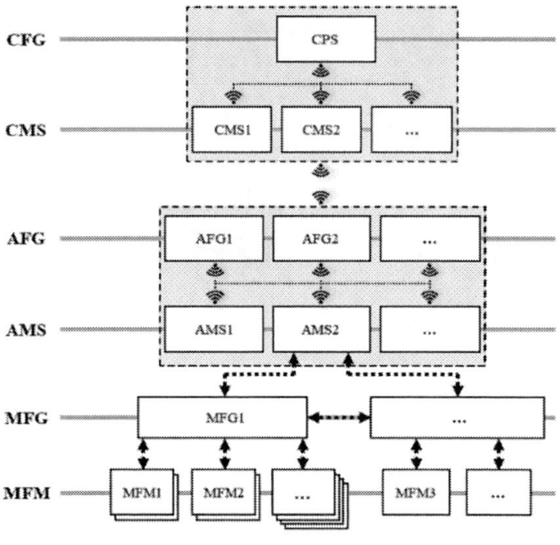

Figure 2. Hierarchical system structure of a CPS on six hierarchical levels [27].

III. DEVELOPMENT OF THE DECENTRALIZED COOPERTIAVE INTERSECTION MANAGEMENT

In this section, the requirements for decentralized cooperative intersection management are collected and defined. Based on this, the system and functional structure as well as the interfaces for integration with other functional modules of an autonomous vehicle in networked traffic systems are designed.

A. Definition of the requirements

Based on the mechatronic development methodology, the requirements for defining the function and structure in the form of requirement specifications and specifications are necessary on the one hand. On the other hand, the requirements are used as a benchmark in the functional validation as well as evaluation of the simulation results [28]. Therefore, based on the analysis of the state of knowledge and the intended scope of application at unsignalized intersections, the following essential requirements for a decentralized cooperative intersection management are defined:

- All road users must proceed through the intersection without collisions and, at the same time, the efficiency in terms of intersection throughput is to be optimized.
- The potential conflicts, especially the dynamic conflicts between vehicles, must be identified early and avoided by appropriate measures.
- For conflict detection, the dynamic traffic information (e.g., direction of travel, current vehicle position and operating conditions) must be continuously updated and transmitted to the concerned road users.
- In case of a conflict between the target criteria e.g., safety and efficiency, it must be ensured that safe driving is always guaranteed.
- The technical constraints regarding the dynamic and kinetic driving behaviours (e.g., available powertrain and braking forces, maximum speed, safety distance) and legal limitations (e.g., maximum speed in urban areas) must be observed during the optimization and a feasible optimum must be defined within their framework.
- The real-time capability and reliability of the intersection management must be guaranteed in any case. I.e., the intersection management must provide a reliable solution within a certain period that allows vehicles to cross the intersection without collisions.
- The universality of the intersection management should not be affected by the topological characteristics of the intersections. Intersection management shall be adaptable to different scenarios and capable of achieving cooperative objectives.
- The intersection management must dynamically adapt to the changing traffic environment (e.g., dynamically varying traffic intensity).
- For smooth communication between heterogeneous traffic participants, the data structure of the information to be exchanged, including data type, format, size, etc., must be uniform.

B. Design of the system structure

Based on the defined requirements, the modular and hierarchically arranged system structure of the highly integrated CPS is derived in accordance with the

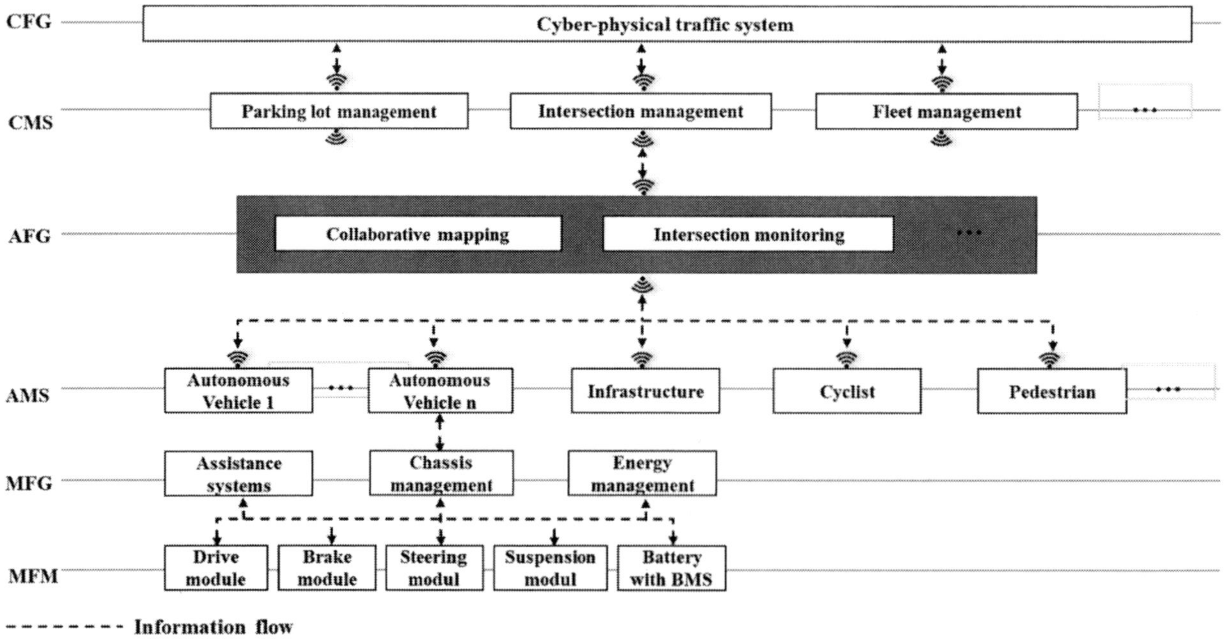

Figure 3. Modular and hierarchical system structure of the CPS.

development methodology for mechatronic structuring in the top-down process, as illustrated in the Fig. 3. Through their highly information integration with each other, a CPS is established at the CFG level.

At the CMS level, it has the management systems to systematically administer the subordinate AMS, which are case-specific developed according to the application areas. The management systems listed work as a central coordinator and strive for a global optimum. Due to the focus of this work, only the intersection management on CMS level and vehicles on AMS level, including the subordinate MFG as well as MFM, are considered here.

Compared to the centralized intersection management at the CMS level, the decentralized intersection management does not play a role as a central coordinator to control AMS, since the vehicles at the AMS level are completely autonomous from their environment in their interconnection. In this case, the decentralized intersection management performs only one task, which is to distribute the information processed and analysed by AFG to the corresponding road users passing through the intersection according to their needs, which enables efficient information provision. In addition, decentralized intersection management enables AMS to communicate with other CMS or even with the highest hierarchy level CFG across system boundaries.

The underlying AFGs are AFG "Collaborative Mapping" and "Intersection Monitoring". Here, the collected data from the sensors installed at the intersection or the information acquired via V2X communication is analysed, resulting in a panorama of the traffic environment, and obtaining new insights by fusing the data from different sources in different dimensions, and thus road users can make reasonable decisions with the comprehensive information. The AFG "Collaborative Map Generation" provides up-to-date and dynamic map data for all vehicles by highly dynamically integrating information provided via V2X communications, such as the direction of travel, vehicle position and operating states of individual road users, with static, highly accurate reference map to complete them. AFG "Intersection Monitoring" is used to collect information on the status of all road users in impact, to detect potential conflicts at an early stage, and to warn road users of the need for action. The information collected can also be used as a basis for decision-making for subsequent enforcement of traffic regulations and clarification of liability.

At the AMS level, all road users in the considered scenario of decentralized intersection management are networked with each other, while in the context of this work this is limited only to autonomous vehicles. The information processing of the AMS "Autonomous Vehicle" includes the "Status Acquisition" as well as "Communication Module" and disposes the information concerning the whole system. Based on this information, the upper-level commands are translated by the MFG-level functional modules into specific action instructions, which are executed by the lower-level MFM-level functional modules.

The functional groups of an autonomous vehicle at MFG level includes MFG "Assistance Systems", "Chassis Management" and "Energy Management". The assistance Systems are used as a combination of the intelligent functions to represent the human drivers in decision making for vehicle guidance. This mainly includes the route guidance to determine an optimal route to a selected destination and the trajectory planning of an optimized driving operation considering the dynamic driving environment based on the selected route [29]. The chassis management refers to the vehicle dynamics control to maintain the desired driving operation (target trajectory), where the target values of the basic driving functions drive, steering, suspension, and braking are determined and issued to the corresponding functional modules [30]. Energy management is used to

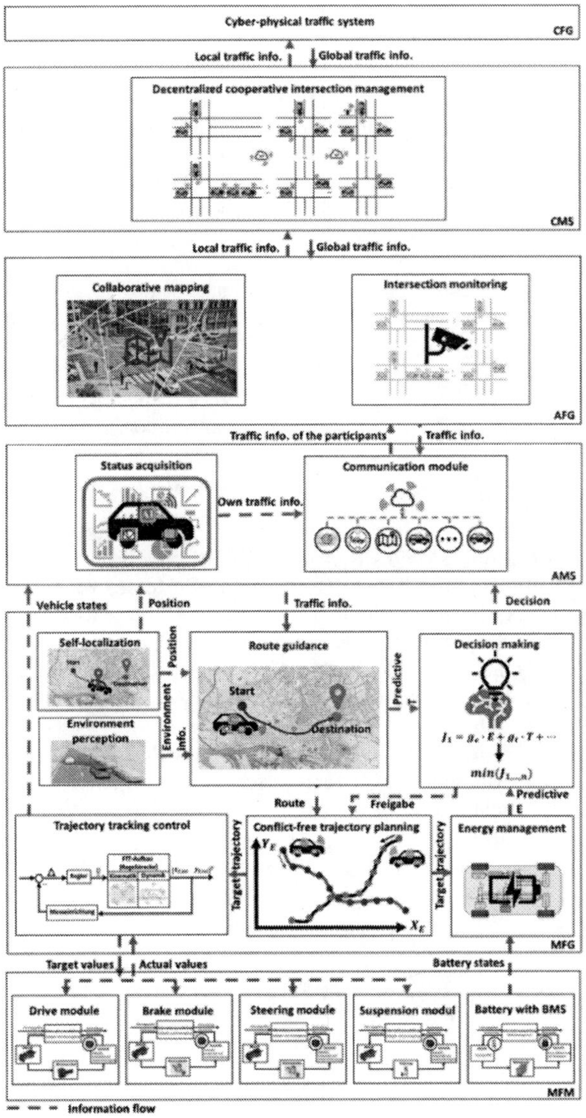

Figure 4. Functional structure of the CPS.

provide the necessary power to operate all mandatory, safety-relevant systems and optionally desirable comfort systems in the vehicle, as well as support for decision-making for vehicle guidance [31].

At the MFM level, in addition to the MFM for implementing the driving behaviour, it has a module for electrical energy supply, which includes a battery module as energy storage and battery management system (BMS) for monitoring the cell states and balancing during charging and discharging.

C. *Design of the functional structure and interfaces*

Form the system structure, the functional structure (cf. Fig. 4) is used to describe the information flow between the functional modules in vertical as well as horizontal directions, which serves as a basis for model description of the studied CPS in virtual test bench.

IV. Function Validation via MiL-Simulations

In this section, the functionality of the developed intersection management is validated and evaluated with an application scenario under different traffic intensity. Subsequently, its generalizability is verified by applying it to a road network consisting of four intersections.

A. *Simulation scenario*

Fig. 5 represents the application scenario in which the autonomous vehicles are considered as the sole mobile road user and can perform the vehicle guidance independently without the intervention of a human driver. The simulation scenario of the CPS is reproduced with respect to the listed parameters in Table I in virtual test bench and the parameters of the vehicle model are adjusted.

B. *Analysis of the simulation results*

To verify the decentralized intersection management, the CPS is modeled and simulated with different traffic intensity in the virtual test bench. Here, the traffic intensity of motor vehicles in the peak hour is divided into three classes based on the class model of Federal Highway Research Institute (BASt) and simulated, whereby the traffic flow at each entrance in the simulation scenario flows evenly into the intersection:

- Low traffic intensity: < 1000 vehicles/h
- Medium traffic intensity: 1000 vehicles/h -2600 vehicles/h

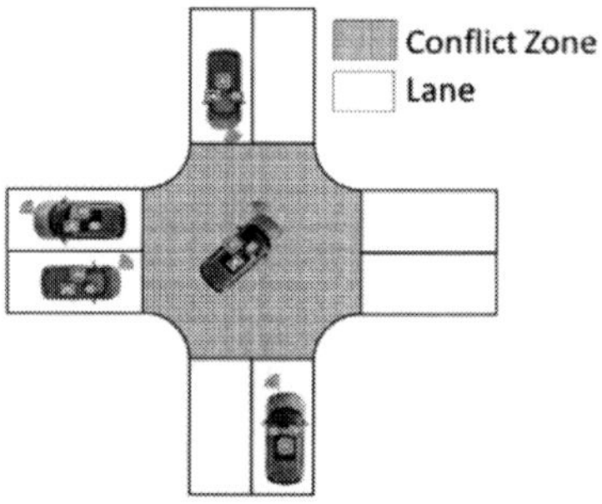

Figure 5. Simulation scenario – single intersection

TABLE I. Parameters for describing the simulation scenario

Intersection	
Width of the lane [m]	4
Width of the conflict zone [m]	24
Vehicle model	
Vehicle length [m]	4
Width of the vehicle [m]	1,9
Max. Acceleration [m/s^2]	4,5
Max. Brake [m/s^2]	10
Max. Velocity [km/h]	50

TABLE II. Analysis of simulation results with regular traffic intensity

Traffic intensity [vehicles/h]	720	2000	3600	7200
$\bar{v}_{init}$ [km/h]	43,5	43,4	43,4	43,1
$\bar{v}_{i\_k}$ [km/h]]	46,1	46,4	46,5	40,0
$\bar{v}_{k}$ [km/h]]	47,7	47,9	47,9	43,1
$\bar{v}_{o\_k}$ [km/h]]	49,2	49,3	49,4	46,2
$\bar{t}_{k}$ [s]	1,5	1,5	1,5	1,6
$\frac{\bar{v}_{i\_k}-\bar{v}_{init}}{\bar{v}_{init}}$ [%]	6,0	7,0	7,1	-7,8
$\frac{\bar{v}_{k}-\bar{v}_{init}}{\bar{v}_{init}}$ [%]	9,6	10,3	10,4	-0,6
$\frac{\bar{v}_{o\_k}-\bar{v}_{init}}{\bar{v}_{init}}$ [%]	13,2	13,6	13,6	6,5
$\frac{\bar{v}_{o\_k}-\bar{v}_{i\_k}}{\bar{v}_{i\_k}}$ [%]	6,8	6,2	6,1	15,5

TABLE III. Analysis of simulation results with irregular traffic intensity

East-West traffic intensity [vehicles/h]	576	1600	2880	5760
North-south traffic intensity [vehicles/h]	288	800	1440	2880
$\bar{v}_{init}$ [km/h]]	43,5	43,5	43,5	43,2
$\bar{v}_{i\_k}$ [km/h]]	43,0	42,0	36,5	25,1
$\bar{v}_{k}$ [km/h]]	46,6	46,0	44,2	36,3
$\bar{v}_{o\_k}$ [km/h]]	50,0	49,9	49,9	48,5
$\bar{t}_{k}$ [s]	1,6	1,7	1,8	2,3
$\frac{\bar{v}_{i\_k}-\bar{v}_{init}}{\bar{v}_{init}}$ [%]	-1,0	-3,5	-15,9	-41,8
$\frac{\bar{v}_{k}-\bar{v}_{init}}{\bar{v}_{init}}$ [%]	7,3	5,8	1,6	-16,0
$\frac{\bar{v}_{o\_k}-\bar{v}_{init}}{\bar{v}_{init}}$ [%]	15,1	14,8	14,8	12,2
$\frac{\bar{v}_{o\_k}-\bar{v}_{i\_k}}{\bar{v}_{i\_k}}$ [%]	16,3	19,0	36,6	92,9

- High traffic intensity: > 2600 vehicles/h

During the simulation, the speed profile of each vehicle crossing the intersection is recorded separately, in particular the initial velocity v_{init}, the velocity entering the conflict zone v_{i_k}, the average velocity in the conflict zone $\bar{v}_{o\_k}$ and the velocity leaving the conflict zone v_{o_k}. Fig. 6 shows the speed change of the ten vehicles with vehicle ID from 51 to 60 when crossing the intersection with traffic intensity of 3600 vehicles/h. For intuitive evaluation of the decentralized intersection management, the simulation results with different traffic volumes are analyzed quantitatively and the main variables to represent the performance of the intersection management according to the target criteria are summarized in Table II.

It is obvious that when the traffic flow is less than 3600 vehicles/h, there is not much difference between the corresponding data sets obtained from the different traffic flow simulations, since the traffic flow at the intersection is regular and there is no congestion. However, when the traffic flow is increased to 7200 vehicles/h, it becomes clear that vehicles must slow down or even to zero before entering the conflict zone due to the congestion at the intersection, so the higher priority vehicles that are already in the conflict zone can pass the conflict zone first, and the conflict zone remains open. By comparing the vehicle velocity at traffic intensity of 7200 vehicles/h and 3600 vehicles/h (cf. Fig. 6 and Fig. 7), the difference becomes particularly obvious. Therefore, the average velocity when entering the conflict zone is about

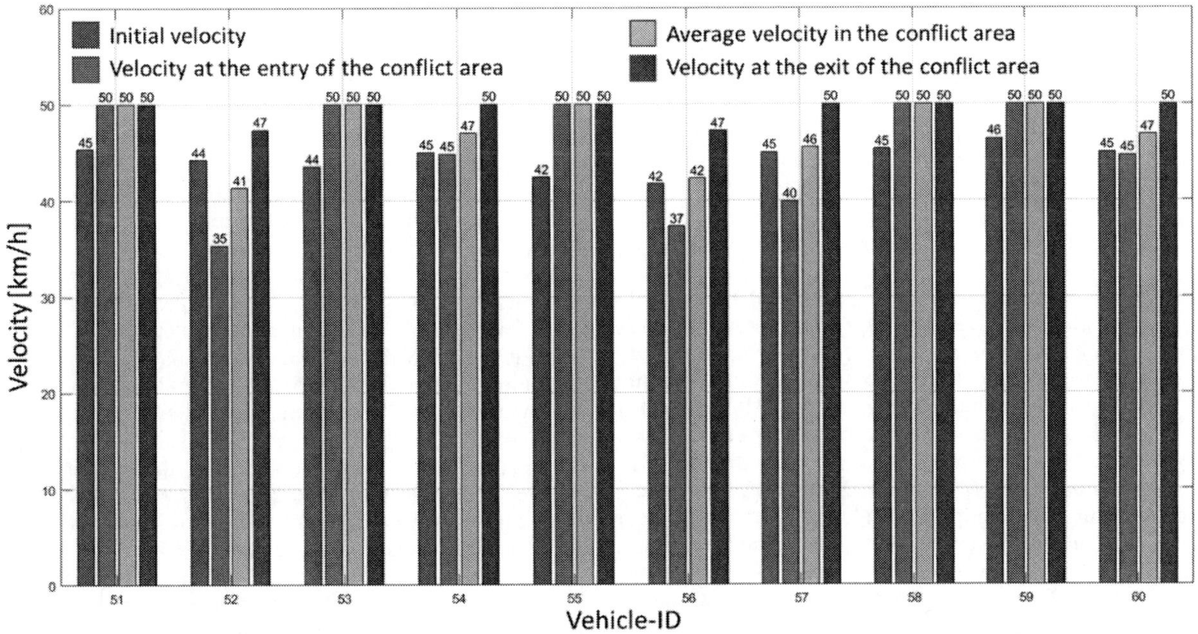

Figure 6. Velocity of vehicles crossing the intersection with a traffic intensity of 3600 vehicles/h.

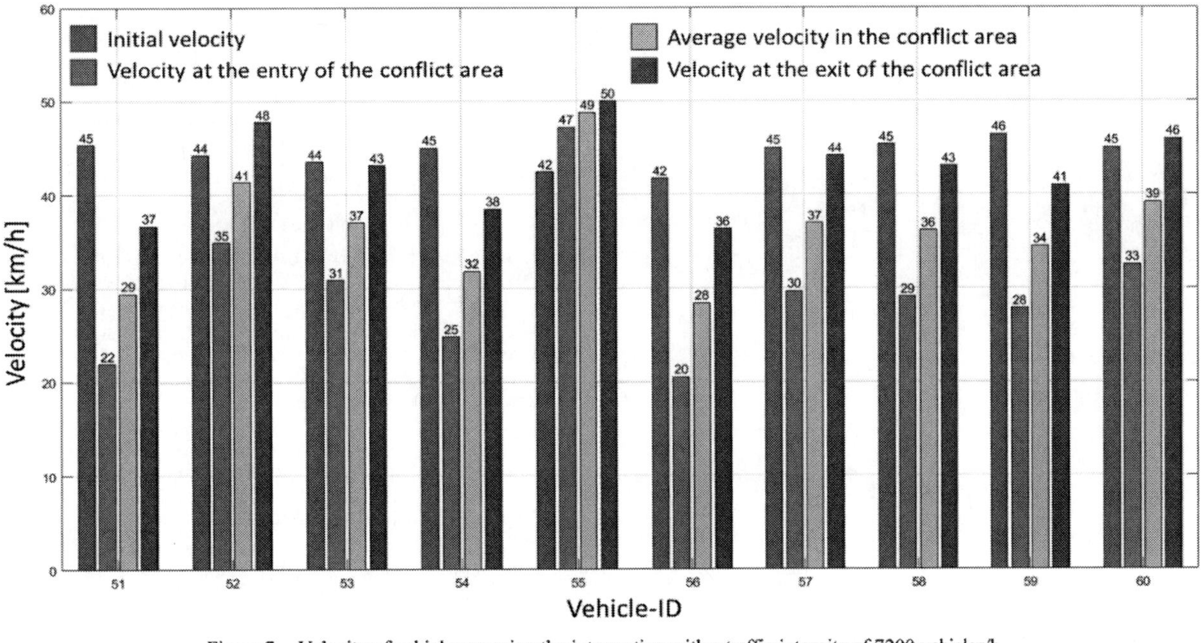

Figure 7. Velocity of vehicles crossing the intersection with a traffic intensity of 7200 vehicles/h.

7.8% lower than the initial average velocity of the vehicles. The average velocity in the conflict zone is increased compared to the average velocity by entering the conflict zone, and vehicles can accelerate through the conflict zone, which is mainly reflected by the fact that the average velocity of vehicles leaving the conflict zone is about 15.5% higher than the average velocity of vehicles entering the conflict zone, and this increase is almost 2.5 times higher than that in the congestion-free circumstance. This shows that decentralized intersection management based on the synergistic cooperation of networked autonomous vehicles can ensure smooth operation of the intersection even under extremely heavy traffic.

Since the traffic intensity at intersections is not regular in all directions, the robustness of the management system should be further investigated when the traffic intensity varies greatly in different directions. Therefore, the intersection management with irregular traffic intensity in different entry directions is researched, and the traffic intensity in east-west direction should be twice as high as that in north-south direction. The essential system parameters are summarized after analysis in Table III. By comparing the cases of regular and irregular traffic intensities in different entry directions, it is found that uneven traffic flow affects the throughput at the intersection. It can also be seen that the average speed at the entrance $\bar{v}_{i\_k}$ is reduced in comparison to the average initial speed $\bar{v}_{init}$ even with low traffic volume, with the drop in $\bar{v}_{i\_k}$ being more pronounced with increasing traffic volume. This is because the vehicles in the lanes with higher traffic intensity have priority by passing through the conflict zone to avoid congestion in the conflict zone, resulting in vehicles in the lanes with lower traffic intensity slowing down when approaching the conflict area reduce or even slow down to zero. However, as soon as the vehicle is in the conflict zone, it accelerates and the average speed $\bar{v}_{o_k}$with which the vehicles leave the conflict area at different traffic volumes is close to the maximum permissible velocity of 50 km/h to keep the traffic flow in the conflict zone fluid.

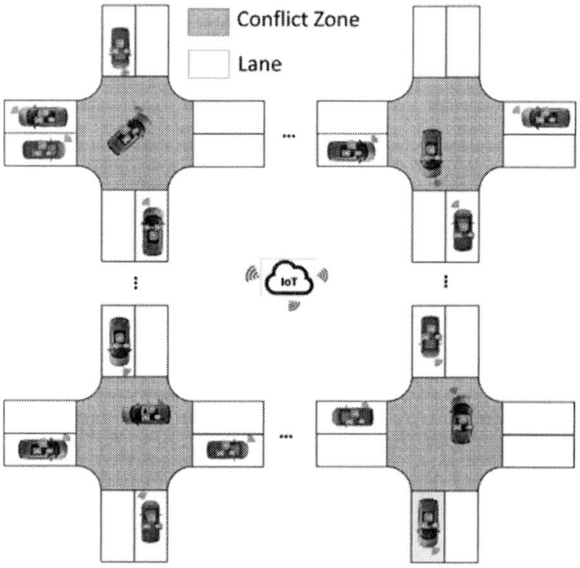

Figure 8. Simulation scenario - road network with four intersections.

To verify the generalization capability of the developed decentralized intersection management, a complex road network consisting of four intersections that are 200 m apart and with different traffic volumes is simulated, as illustrated in Fig. 8. The simulation results proved that the intersection management is also suitable for road networks with multiple intersections.

V. Conclusion

In this paper, the decentralized cooperative intersection management system by means of networked autonomous vehicles is designed and developed to optimize traffic throughput and ensure proactive traffic safety. Based on the defined requirements, the system and functional structure of the studied CPS is created, and then modelled in the virtual test bed and simulated with different traffic intensity, where the traffic intensity can be regular or irregular in different entry directions. The functionality of the intersection management is validated and quantitatively evaluated with the support of MiL simulation. By integrating the intersection management into a road network, the generalizability is verified.

In the next steps, the general applicability of the developed intersection management system can be used in intersections with different topological characteristics and verified by simulation. By comparing and evaluating the performance of centralized and decentralized intersection management with different traffic intensity, a new mechanism of intersection management will be developed, which dynamically adapts to the traffic flow by switching centralized and decentralized approaches to achieve the best performance.

Acknowledgment

Funded by the Lower Saxony Ministry of Science and Culture under grant number ZN3495 within the Lower Saxony "Vorab" of the Volkswagen Foundation and supported by the Center for Digital Innovations (ZDIN).

References

[1] J. Broughton et al., “Traffic safety basic facts 2012: junctions,” 2013. Accessed January 30, 2023. [retrieved: January, 2023]: http://hdl.handle.net/10550/30218.

[2] NHTSA, “Fatality Analysis Reporting System (FARS),” Washington, DC, USA, 2020. [retrieved: January, 2023]: https://www.nhtsa.gov/crash-data-systems/fatality-analysis-reporting-system.

[3] L. Wei, Z. Li, J. Gong, C. Gong, and J. Li, “Autonomous Driving Strategies at Intersections: Scenarios, State-of-the-Art, and Future Outlooks,” 2021 IEEE International Intelligent Transportation Systems Conference (ITSC), 2021, pp. 44-51, doi: 10.1109/ITSC48978.2021.9564518.

[4] German Insurers Accident Research (UDV), “Dutch-style intersections worsen visibility for trucks”. 2020. [retrieved: January, 2023]: https://www.udv.de/udv/themen/kreuzungen-nach-niederlaendischem-vorbild-verschlechtert-sicht-fuer-lkw-81518.

[5] A. Gholamhosseinian and J. Seitz, "A Comprehensive Survey on Cooperative Intersection Management for Heterogeneous Connected Vehicles," in IEEE Access, vol. 10, pp. 7937-7972, 2022, doi: 10.1109/ACCESS.2022.3142450.

[6] E. Namazi, J. Li, and C. Lu, "Intelligent Intersection Management Systems Considering Autonomous Vehicles: A Systematic Literature Review," in IEEE Access, vol. 7, pp. 91946-91965, 2019, doi: 10.1109/ACCESS.2019.2927412.

[7] C. Zhao et al., "A comparative study of state-of-the-art driving strategies for autonomous vehicles," Accident Analysis & Prevention, vol. 150, p. 105937, 2021/02/01/ 2021.

[8] L. Wei, Z. Li, J. Gong, C. Gong, and J. Li, "Autonomous Driving Strategies at Intersections: Scenarios, State-of-the-Art, and Future Outlooks," 2021 IEEE International Intelligent Transportation Systems Conference (ITSC), Indianapolis, IN, USA, 2021, pp. 44-51, doi: 10.1109/ITSC48978.2021.9564518.

[9] W. Luo, "Research on Model and Algorithm of Traffic Flow Control on Intersection under the Background of Intelligent Transportation," [Dissertation], 2018, Beijing Jiaotong University.

[10] V.L. Knoop, H.J. Zuylen, and S.P. Hoogendoorn, "Microscopic Traffic Behaviour near Incidents," Springer Books, in: William H. K. Lam & S. C. Wong & Hong K. Lo (ed.), Transportation and Traffic Theory 2009: Golden Jubilee, pp. 75-97, Springer.

[11] L. Chen and C. Englund, "Cooperative Intersection Management: A Survey," in IEEE Transactions on Intelligent Transportation Systems, vol. 17, no. 2, pp. 570-586, Feb. 2016, doi: 10.1109/TITS.2015.2471812.

[12] M.A.S. Kamal, J.-i. Imura, T. Hayakawa, A. Ohata, and K. Aihara, "A Vehicle-Intersection Coordination Scheme for Smooth Flows of Traffic Without Using Traffic Lights," in IEEE Transactions on Intelligent Transportation Systems, vol. 16, no. 3, pp. 1136-1147, June 2015, doi: 10.1109/TITS.2014.2354380.

[13] H. Xu, Y. Zhang, L. Li, and W. Li, "Cooperative driving at unsignalized intersections using tree search," IEEE Transactions on Intelligent Transportation Systems, vol. 21, no. 11, pp. 4563-4571, 2020.

[14] J. Gregoire, "Priority-based coordination of mobile robots," arXiv preprint arXiv:1410.0879, 2014.

[15] T. Zhou, H. Zhao, Y. Wang, and J. Yang, "A multi-vehicles optimization method for intersection cooperative driving," in 2017 29th Chinese Control And Decision Conference (CCDC), 2017, pp. 5855-5861.

[16] J. Zhang and X. Liu-Henke, "Optimal Dispatching of Transport Orders Using Genetic Algorithm for Decentralized Order Management System of AGVs," The 2021 IEEE International Conference on Recent Advances in Systems Science and Engineering (RASSE2021), Online, December 12-14, 2021.

[17] H. Xu, Y. Zhang, L. Li, and W. Li, "Kooperatives Fahren an unsignalisierten Kreuzungen mit Baumsuche," in IEEE Transactions on Intelligent Transportation Systems , vol. 21, no. 11, pp. 4563-4571, Nov. 2020, doi: 10.1109/TITS.2019.2940641.

[18] X. Chen, Y. Sun, Y. Ou, X. Zheng, Z. Wang, and M. Li, "A conflict decision model based on game theory for intelligent vehicles at urban unsignalized intersections," IEEE Access, vol. 8, pp. 189546-189555, 2020.

[19] Z. Yang, H. Huang, G. Wang, X. Pei, and Y. Danya, "Cooperative driving model for non-signalized intersections with cooperative games," Journal of Central South University, vol. 25, no. 9, pp.2164-2181, 2018/09/01 2018.

[20] X. Zhao, J. Wang, G. Yin, and K. Zhang, "Cooperative Driving for Connected and Automated Vehicles at Non-signalized Intersection based on Model Predictive Control," 2019 IEEE Intelligent Transportation Systems Conference (ITSC), Auckland, New Zealand, 2019, pp. 2121-2126, doi: 10.1109/ITSC.2019.8916786.

[21] A.I.M. Medina, N. Wouw, and H. Nijmeijer, "Cooperative intersection control based on virtual platooning," IEEE Transactions on Intelligent Transportation Systems, vol. 19, no. 6, pp. 1727-1740, 2018.

[22] H. Xu, Y. Zhang, L. Li, and W. Li, "Cooperative driving at unsignalized intersections using tree search," IEEE Transactions on Intelligent Transportation Systems, vol. 21, no. 11, pp. 4563-4571, 2020.

[23] Y. Zhang and C.G. Cassandras, "A Decentralized Optimal Control Framework for Connected Automated Vehicles at Urban Intersections with Dynamic Resequencing," 2018 IEEE Conference on Decision and Control (CDC), 2018, pp. 217-222, doi: 10.1109/CDC.2018.8618871.

[24] H. Pei, Y. Zhang, Q. Tao, S. Feng, and L. Li, "Distributed Cooperative Driving in Multi-Intersection Road Networks," in IEEE Transactions on Vehicular Technology, vol. 70, no. 6, pp. 5390-5403, June 2021, doi: 10.1109/TVT.2021.3079272.

[25] D. Inkermann et al., "An integrated framework to classify Industry 4.0 technologies within production and product development," 29th CIRP Design Conference, Póvoa de Varzim, Portugal, May 08 - 10, 2019.

[26] J. Lückel, X. Liu-Henke and T. Hestermeyer, "Generalization of the Cascade Principle in View of a Structured Form of Mechatronic Systems," IEEE/ASME International Conference on Advanced Intelligent Mechatronics (AIM '01), Como, Italien, 2001.

[27] X. Liu-Henke, S. Jacobitz, S. Scherler, M. Göllner, O. Yarom, and J. Zhang, "A Holistic Methodology for Model-Based Design of Mechatronic Systems in Digitized and Connected System Environments," 16th International Conference on Software Technologies (ICSOFT), Online, July 6-8, 2021.

[28] D. Inkermann et al., "Model-Based Requirement Engineering to Support Development of Complex Systems," Procedia CIRP, 84, pp. 239-244, 2019 doi: 10.1016/j.procir.2019.04.345.

[29] J. Zhang, O. Yarom, and X. Liu-Henke, "Decentralized, self-optimized order-acceptance decision of autonomous guided vehicles in an IoT-based production facility," International Journal of Mechanical Engineering and Robotics Research (IJMERR), vol. 10, no. 1, January, 2021.

[30] J. Zhang and X. Liu-Henke, "Model-based design of the vehicle dynamics control for an omnidirectional automated guided vehicle (AGV)," 15th International Conference Mechatronic Systems and Materials (MSM2020), Bialystok, Poland, July 1-3, 2020.

[31] S. Scherler, X. Liu-Henke and M. Henke, "Predictive Energy Management for an Electric Vehicle with Fuel Cell Range Extender in Connected Traffic Systems," 19th IEEE-Mechatronika 2020, Prague, Czech Republic, December 2 - 4 2020.

A Multi-dimensional Analysis to Societal Resilience in Context of COVID-19: A Systems Thinking Approach

Bijun Wang
School of System and Enterprises
Stevens Institute of Technology
Hoboken, NJ USA
e-mail: bwang27@stevens.edu

Mo Mansouri
School of System and Enterprises
Stevens Institute of Technology
Hoboken, NJ USA
e-mail: mmansour@stevens.edu

Onur Asan
School of System and Enterprises
Stevens Institute of Technology
Hoboken, NJ USA
e-mail: oasan@stevens.edu

Abstract—**The COVID-19 pandemic has highlighted the importance of system resilience in confronting major crises. This paper leverages the systems thinking approach to emphasize the interactions and feedback among systems for fostering resilience from multiple levels and timing stages. This paper also emphasizes the impact of socio-technical systems on societal resilience, since it is a crucial aspect of resilience and is discussed in terms of its ability to disseminate information, policies, and promote system resourcefulness and flexibility. In addition, we analyze the interrelationships and interactions among systems at multiple levels, including macro-level (society), meso-level (community and local network), and micro-level (individual and families), to foster resilience from different angles. We also review policies that correspond to different spatial-temporal resilience stages (preparation, disturbance, recovery, transformation) to provide enlightenment for policymaking from a resilience thinking perspective. Our analysis reveals that a system's resilience relies on the interconnectedness and feedback mechanism among systems, and policy design should aim to minimize functionality loss in the shortest time to maintain robustness and rapidity in response. Additionally, the dynamic and unpredictable nature of the transformation process should be taken into account when implementing policies at different levels. Our study can serve as a future research path aiming at enhancing societal resilience in facing the challenges and preparing for potential pandemics in the future.**

Keywords- resilience; systems thinking; complex system; COVID-19; healthcare system; governance system; socio-technical system.

I. INTRODUCTION

The COVID-19 has triggered a global systemic crisis that reveals the vulnerability, fragility and uncertainty of the societal system at the beginning of the pandemic. While the end of the pandemic may be in sight, its variants will likely continue to coexist with society for a long time [1][2]. As we continue to study COVID-19, it has become clear the pandemic is not just a public health problem, but a social problem that requires effort from every aspect of the societal system to respond to the crisis. In this paper, we will discuss how to deal with COVID-19 and recover societal resilience from a systems thinking viewpoint in both the current and post-pandemic era.

The outbreak of the COVID-19 pandemic and the resulting systemic crisis have affected almost everyone [3][4]. Given that we cannot avoid all risks, a new subject arises: what can be done to minimize disruption and damage, and restore social order with adaptivity, diversity, and stability? Severe disruptions like these prompt us to consider how we handle interruptions, withstand threats, and adapt to adverse situations in the future, at different levels. As a result, the concept of "resilience" has received considerable attention in the context of COVID-19 and the complex systems approach. The term "resilience" derives from the Latin word meaning "bounce back" [6], and it was initially used in ecosystems to enhance stability and sustainability by conserving biodiversity [1][7].

In recent years, resilience has been well developed and adapted to different societal system sectors such as socio-ecology, socio-economic, socio-technology, and socio-science [8]. In broad terms, system resilience refers to the ability of a complex system to return to pre-existing equilibrium better, with redundancy, after experiencing a crisis. It involves the capacity of individuals, families, or even the whole society to prepare, respond, absorb, adapt, and minimize the negative impact of the crisis [9][10]. For complex adaptive systems, resilience can be seen as the inherent property of the system [2] that represents a process by which complex systems absorb negative impacts from stress and disruption and improve functionality properly. Importantly, system resilience is not a transient state that causes deviation in functioning or behavior. Rather, it is a process by which a system can cope with disruption and adapt from crisis to transformation [11]. By understanding resilience in this way, we can better prepare and respond to crises like COVID-19, and ultimately, enhance the resilience of our societal systems.

The rest of the paper is structured as follows. In section II, this study employs a systems thinking approach to analyze interactions and feedback among systems in addressing the COVID-19 pandemic to get a holistic understanding of systemic resilience. Section III emphasizes the role of socio-technical systems in societal resilience. In section IV, we examine interrelationships at macro, meso, and micro levels, and explore how these interactions impact resilience across different stages and sectors. In section V, our research then reviews policies for various spatial-temporal resilience stages, offering insights for policy development and enhancing societal resilience against future pandemics. The conclusions close the article. By utilizing systems thinking, we facilitate scalable and appropriate policy implementation in decision-making processes, incorporating dynamic and feedback control. Our study contributes to current resilience research in complex system sectors, aiming to tackle crises effectively.

II. Complexity of Systemic Resilience

A. Resilience: More Than a Single System Feature

The complex societal system implies that the world changes non-linearly and is composed of massively interconnected systems and networks [14]. The continued evolution of resilience originates from the interaction and interdependency of systems and environments [15][16]. Dynamic relationships are challenging to identify [17], whereas linearity usually cannot be used to describe interconnections and interactions within systems or to reflect the emergent properties of the complex societal system [3], [4]. Thus, we must re-examine the importance of resilience in complex systems, especially given the ongoing impact of the COVID-19 and its variants. Overlooking the interconnectedness of resilience between systems will significantly increase the vulnerabilities of a systemic shock [5].

While enhancing and developing system integration has led to closely paired systems that improve efficiency and effectiveness in normal conditions [18], advanced technologies applied in continuously evolving systems with tight connections may result in negative effects being mapped onto other systems and causing a disruption of balance and normalcy [19]. Our tendency to target the most apparent problems without considering broader implications can lead to unforeseen consequences. For instance, the implementation of strict policies may overlook the complexity and interaction of the global economy and transportation, resulting in the creation of new social problems that accumulate over time [2].

B. Resilience: Facing The Interactions and Collectivity in The Dynamic World

Moreover, even the resilience reflected in a single system may manifest in different ways, both within and beyond the system [20]. For example, the resilience of the healthcare system usually interweaves with the economic system, supply chain system, governance system and other related systems. A typical phenomenon is that during the early period of the pandemic, the healthcare system is not functioning properly due to the shortage of supplies, which is highly reliant on the supply chain and transportation system. At the same time, the supply chain and transportation system are highly dependent on the labor force, which increases the chance of massive transmission if they go back to work too soon, increasing the complexity of policymaking and pressure on the healthcare system [21]. System complexity can prompt societal development, but it can also cascade adverse effects, leading to system failure counterintuitively. Thus, it is essential to consider the interconnectedness of different systems in developing and implementing resilient policies.

Considering the close intertwined problems from a complex systems viewpoint, society can be understood as a whole but structured into different systems based on societal elements and related factors and subsystems, such as the governance system, epidemiological factors, human activity, healthcare system, socio-technical system, and infrastructure system [4][20][22]. Multi-systems and factors of society are involved at various scales, as shown in Figure 1. In such a

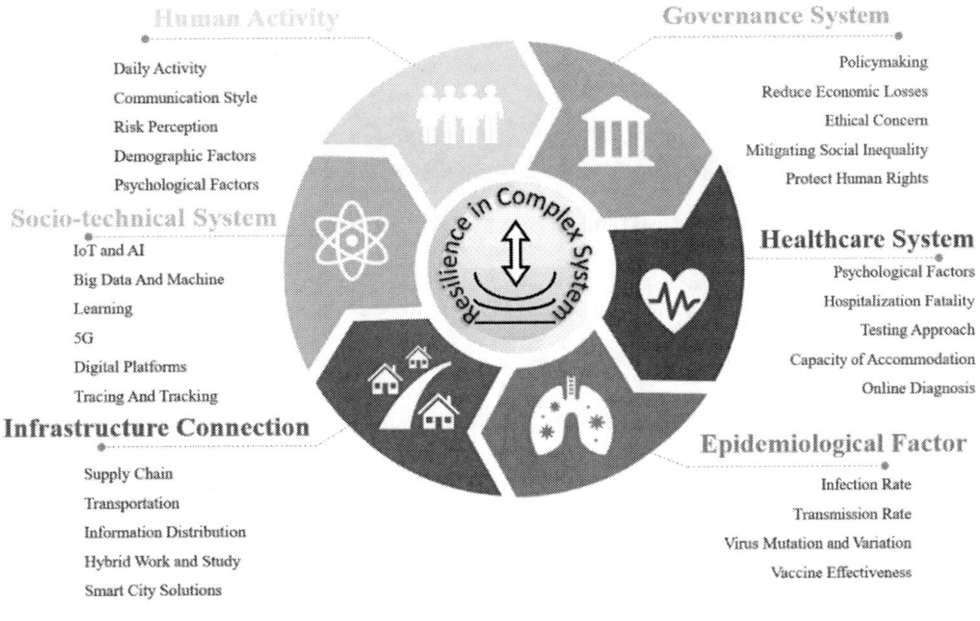

Figure 1. The interconnections and interactions in Complex societal system resilience facing to COVID-19

complex societal system, system resilience is driven by both positive and negative outcomes, such as sudden changes or crises and the adaptation of new features, which can shape the complex system and impact resilience at different sectors and levels [15][22].

III. The Role of Socio-technical System Resilience Under COVID-19

A. Socio-technical System Aligned with the Concept of Society 5.0

The COVID-19 is different from previous global crises because it happened after the integration of human-technology interactions at the organizational or societal level. [17]. Therefore, we emphasize the role of the socio-technical system in systemic resilience, which indirectly affects the virus spread through information dissemination, policy implementation, and behavior change. The socio-technical system can be identified as the combination of human-centered systems and technological systems [18]. Currently, the socio-technical system can be viewed as a complex system formed by the fusion of virtual and physical elements and components interacting with subsystems in society such as education, transportation, and healthcare system in society, affecting people's daily life and decision-making process for stakeholders [10][19].

The concept of Society 5.0 integrates society, human factors, and technology within a broader perspective, emphasizing the interrelatedness of functionalities within the societal system [19]. With the shift to Society 5.0, the socio-technical system has become increasingly significant for ensuring system resilience, particularly for identifying and addressing heterogeneous threats. The socio-technical system is embedded within the societal system and interacts with multifaceted systems to make flexible and adaptive decisions, ensuring cohesion and resilience in fast-changing environments. The hyper-connectivity and communicability of different systems in the complex societal network allow them to be cascaded like nodes in a network, creating feedback loops characterized by interdependent and communicative systems, which serve as an essential layer to support system resilience.

B. The Impact of Socio-technical System on Systemic Resilience

On the one hand, the maturity of the infrastructure system, a result of globalization and urbanization, has accelerated the spread of the virus and negatively impacted societal resilience due to insufficient preparation and policy implementation at the beginning of the pandemic [1]. However, advances in socio-technology have also facilitated the dissemination of information and policies, changing hu-

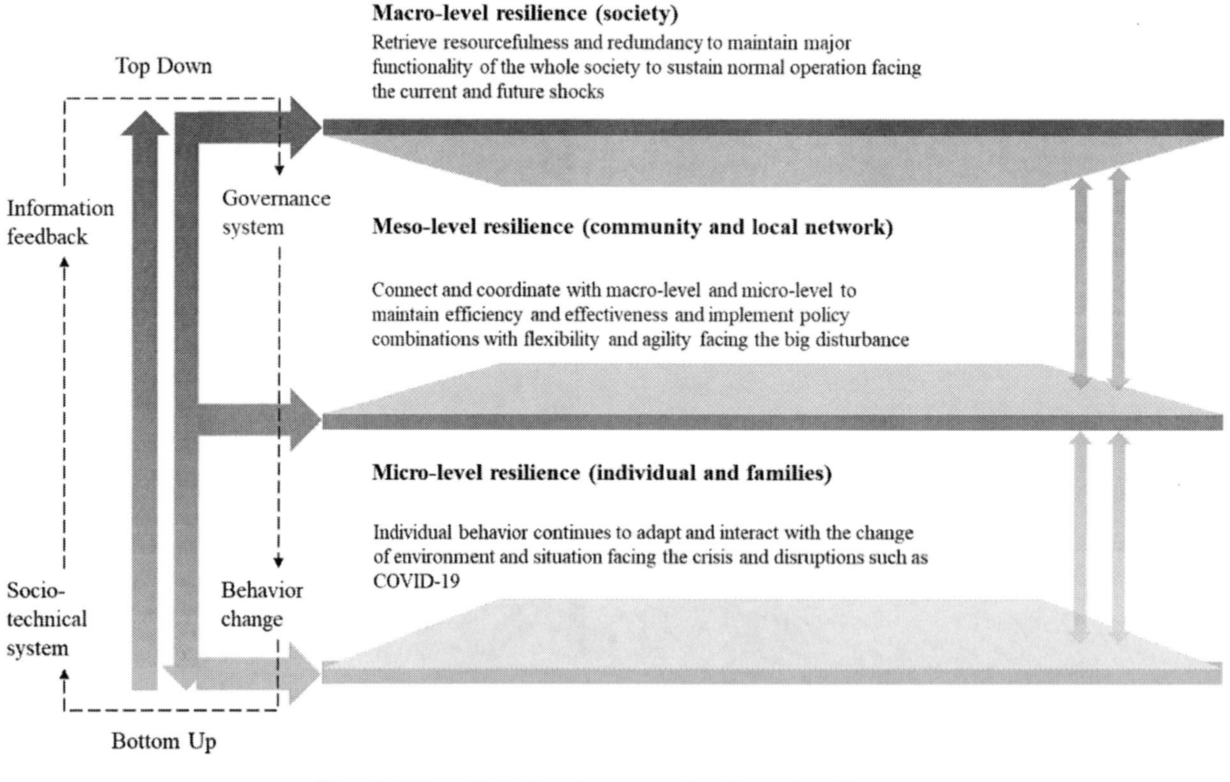

Figure 2. A hierarchical schematic representation of systemic resilience

man behavior and awareness of the current COVID-19 and future crises [19]. The socio-technical system, by involving itself in every stage of the resilience process, promotes system resourcefulness and flexibility to solve difficulties.

On the other hand, technology has played a crucial role in enhancing resilience at individual and systemic levels by enabling innovative risk mitigation methods. For example, increased online connectivity reduces physical encounters, minimizing transmission risk while maintaining daily routines through telemedicine, online education, and remote work [1][3]. Although COVID-19 may temporarily hinder development plans, the long-term outlook remains optimistic, as the crisis drives the creation of more intelligent and resilient societal systems. The socio-technical system improves risk estimation, prediction, communication efficiency, and risk perception abilities, allowing for better understanding of interactions and delays within and among systems.

IV. IDENTIFICATION OF MULTI-LEVEL RESILIENCE FACE COVID-19 PANDEMIC

To gain a deeper understanding of system resilience, we conduct an integrated multi-level analysis, including macro-, meso-, and micro-levels, to visualize the interrelationships and interconnectedness among systems when facing major disasters, as shown in Figure 2 (developed based on [1][4] [15][23]). This collaborative effort is necessary, as the actions taken in one system can have an impact on others in a complex adaptive system. In this section, we aim to illustrate perceived risk, vulnerability, and societal reactions, as well as to discuss the interaction and interconnectedness that cascade across different levels, based on the principles of systems thinking.

A. *Macro-level Resilience*

Macro-level resilience assesses overall system resilience while focusing on the complex interconnected factors that shape the systems' ability to adjust and adapt to traumatic events. During emergencies, macro-level resilience takes the entire society into consideration, performing the function of retrieving resources and redundancy to maintain the major functionality of the whole society and sustain society's major functionalities in the face of current and future shocks [4]. Since the macro layer has access to collect and allocate most resources including information and entities, strategic accumulation retrieves resourcefulness will continually nourish the whole system to have redundancy in crisis management. The governance system intervenes from the top down to guide the meso-level to formulate more flexible and appropriate policies and turn people's behavior towards a healthier and more resilient direction to recover from emergencies. These effects influence the design and implementation of future policies aimed at building a sufficient buffer for any national emergencies. This feedback may be positive or negative due to the various system interactions and interdependencies. Therefore, the macro layer provides a framework to guide the sustainability and resilience of different systems to maximize the well-being of the entire society in the midst of an epidemic.

B. *Meso-level Resilience*

The meso-level of the resilience system serves as a vital connection between macro and micro levels, representing local organizations and communities with some autonomy. This level acts as a strong adhesive and moderator between society and individuals [24]. Policymaking and implementation can be time-consuming, and macro-level restrictions may not immediately restore societal resilience, making meso-level flexibility crucial for policy implementation. In response, the meso-level governance system can adapt to local conditions, targeting operational robustness and agility to improve resilience for future pandemic waves. It cannot be overlooked that a single failure or debilitation in one system, or a negative interaction between systems, can impair systemic resilience from the operational level to the individual level [17]. Resilience at the micro level may emerge from the bottom-up, affecting the ability to absorb and adapt to threats at meso and macro levels. Detailed and flexible governance enables communities and organizations to interpret and implement policies based on their situation, promoting local resilience and ultimately enhancing the entire social system's resilience with the socio-technical system's power to deliver information and receive feedback.

C. *Micro-level Resilience*

In addition to the collective approach to systemic resilience, individual views and perceptions are also crucial in navigating the complexities of the world. The importance of individual and family-level resilience cannot be ignored as they represent the basic and vulnerable units of society [1]. The COVID-19 pandemic has had a significant impact on the mental health and well-being of individuals, exposing their vulnerability and substantial risk. Extended self-quarantine, canceled social events, and social distancing have all significantly affected human well-being [24]. During the early stages of the outbreak, widespread rumors caused by fear of the unknown also had a detrimental effect on mental health [16].

Individual behavior rapidly adapts and interacts with changes in the environment and situation based on the information and guidance provided by the macro-level and meso-level of society. The socio-technical system collects reactions from individuals and provides feedback to the governance system for policy adjustments and improvements, promoting resilience from every aspect of society [19]. Furthermore, individuals may overcome disturbances and adapt their behavior to the changing environment in the post-pandemic era through the benefits of human-centered design. Matured socio-technical systems have created various interaction mechanisms and opportunities to cultivate resilience in individuals.

V. DEEPER THE ANALYSIS: A RESILIENCE MATRIX

COVID-19 unlike discrete events such as tornadoes or earthquakes, has lasted for years with massive and multifaceted interactions among systems. It should be recognized as a complex process within time constraints to

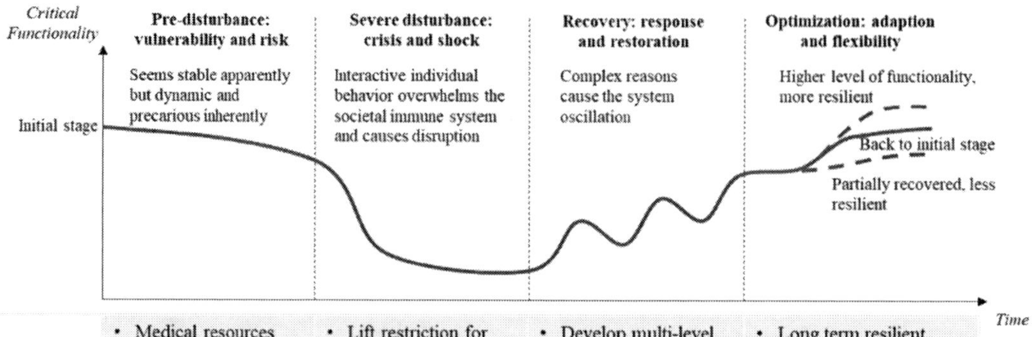

	Pre-disturbance: vulnerability and risk	**Severe disturbance: crisis and shock**	**Recovery: response and restoration**	**Optimization: adaption and flexibility**
Macro-level resilience	• Medical resources reservation • Impact planning and analysis • Healthcare demand estimation • Response planning • See the big picture • Media publication • Public Engagement	• Lift restriction for healthcare • Evidenced decision making • Leverage the power of socio-technical system • Resources distribution • Shorten resolution process during emergency	• Develop multi-level recovery framework • Flexibility in policymaking • Facilitate the business continuity • Enhance public credibility • Support for reopening	• Long term resilient plan • Review and improve related policies • Develop stimulus package • Develop strategies for new waves of disaster • Long-term consideration for society sustainability
Meso-level resilience	• Develop communication channels • Public education • Medication distribution • Information sharing • Essential items restriction • Dispel rumors	• Strong collaboration to connect each layer • Coordinate health facilities, transportation and other sectors • Set up vaccine sites • Prevent large population gathering	• Provide mental health support • Flexibility in policy execution • Monitor and support local vulnerable population • Implementation of recovery framework	• Strengthen community capacity for continues local support • Continue operating key testing site and shelter • Monitor and report the potential new wave of disaster • Psychological health counseling
Micro-level resilience	• Living resources planning • Self-education • Emotional preparation • Maintain good communication with local governance system • Risk perception	• Keep social distance • Increase virtual communications • Volunteer and community support • Protect yourself and families • Online education and work from home	• Preparing for back to work and school • Continue personal safety protocol • Request support for both health and financial difficulties • Psychological adjustment	• Continues recovery of normal life • Caution for potential new wave of disaster • Build new resilience and Learn from disasters • Maintain flexibility and adaptability

Figure 3. Resilience and policymaking matrix during COVID-19 pandemic at different stages

absorb negative impacts and gradually restore functionalities with some newly emergent properties to adapt to changes. Various policy combinations can affect resilience at different levels and degrees, resulting from interactions across different scales of social structure and levels of governance [15]. An accountable and reliable governance system can minimize the impacts of the pandemic. Inspired by the classic resilience curve [2]–[4], this study reviews and outlines implemented policies for different resilience stages (preparation, disturbance, recovery, transformation) across macro-, meso- and micro-levels based on current research on resilience and governance to respond to disturbances and traumatic events, as shown in Figure 3 [3][14][19][20][22][25]. Examining policy implementations from both spatial-temporal dimensions can help stakeholders govern the uncertainty and dynamics in a complex world. The resilience matrix integrates a range of policies across domains such as education, transportation, technology, demographics, healthcare, and social norms related to society, community, and individual resilience change.

Policymaking at different levels must take into account various time stages, not only focusing on immediate policies for immediate results, but also considering long-term resilience. The system must accumulate enough adaptability and robustness to respond to continuous turmoil, and have redundancy and resourcefulness to prevent significant functionality loss. The constant intertwining of systems combined with policymaking also makes the transformation process unpredictable. The system may bounce back to the pre-disaster stage with the initial equilibrium, or it may become more resilient to transformation with higher levels of functionality and creativity. However, some systems may fail to recover or require a long time to restore the function [2] [25]. Thus, in the post-pandemic era, opportunities and crises will coexist, and policymakers must balance short-term and long-term considerations to promote resilience at all levels.

VI. CONCLUSION

In conclusion, this paper highlights the importance of system resilience in disaster management and risk response, using a systems thinking approach to examine multi-level interactions and feedback. By focusing on system interdependencies, we can better identify vulnerabilities and strengths, informing policy for various spatial-temporal resilience stages. Our study aims to promote cross-sectional contributions, enhance societal resilience, and minimize functionality loss during crises, such as the COVID-19 pandemic.

However, our paper does have some limitations, as we could not include detailed case studies to better explain our findings due to space limitations. For future research, we suggest exploring the impact of different policy combinations on resilience across various stages through evidence-based studies. As the COVID-19 pandemic offers a unique opportunity to assess system resilience performance, it provides insights for preparing for future crises.

REFERENCES

[1] N. Zhang, S. Yang, and P. Jia, "Cultivating Resilience During the COVID-19 Pandemic: A Socioecological Perspective," Annual Review of Psychology, vol. 73, no. 1, pp. 575–598, 2022, doi: 10.1146/annurev-psych-030221-031857.

[2] W. Hynes, B. Trump, P. Love, and I. Linkov, "Bouncing forward: a resilience approach to dealing with COVID-19 and future systemic shocks," Environ Syst Decis, vol. 40, no. 2, pp. 174–184, Jun. 2020, doi: 10.1007/s10669-020-09776-x.

[3] B. Wang and M. Mansouri, "Dealing with COVID-19 Pandemic in Complex Societal System for Resilience Study: A Systems Approach," INCOSE International Symposium, vol. 31, no. 1, pp. 649–663, 2021, doi: 10.1002/j.2334-5837.2021.00860.x.

[4] D. A. Behrens, M. S. Rauner, and M. Sommersguter-Reichmann, "Why Resilience in Health Care Systems is More than Coping with Disasters: Implications for Health Care Policy," Schmalenbach J Bus Res, vol. 74, no. 4, pp. 465–495, Dec. 2022, doi: 10.1007/s41471-022-00132-0.

[5] S. Jackson, "6.1.3 System Resilience: Capabilities, Culture and Infrastructure," INCOSE International Symposium, vol. 17, no. 1, pp. 885–899, 2007, doi: 10.1002/j.2334-5837.2007.tb02920.x.

[6] A. Labib, "Towards a new approach for managing pandemics: Hybrid resilience and bowtie modelling," Safety Science, vol. 139, p. 105274, Jul. 2021, doi: 10.1016/j.ssci.2021.105274.

[7] S. Hosseini, K. Barker, and J. E. Ramirez-Marquez, "A review of definitions and measures of system resilience," Reliability Engineering & System Safety, vol. 145, pp. 47–61, Jan. 2016, doi: 10.1016/j.ress.2015.08.006.

[8] J. Amadi-Echendu, L. Ebersöhn, C. du Plessis, A. van der Merwe, and G. Stols, "A Multidisciplinary Case Study on Managing the Resilience of Connected systems," in 2020 IEEE Technology & Engineering Management Conference (TEMSCON), Jun. 2020, pp. 1–6. doi: 10.1109/TEMSCON47658.2020.9140139.

[9] C. S. Holling, "Resilience and Stability of Ecological Systems," Annual Review of Ecology and Systematics, vol. 4, no. 1, pp. 1–23, 1973, doi: 10.1146/annurev.es.04.110173.000245.

[10] D. Gama Dessavre, J. E. Ramirez-Marquez, and K. Barker, "Multidimensional approach to complex system resilience analysis," Reliability Engineering & System Safety, vol. 149, pp. 34–43, May 2016, doi: 10.1016/j.ress.2015.12.009.

[11] B. M. Ayyub, "Systems Resilience for Multihazard Environments: Definition, Metrics, and Valuation for Decision Making," Risk Analysis, vol. 34, no. 2, pp. 340–355, 2014, doi: 10.1111/risa.12093.

[12] B. Wang, S. Xu, and M. Mansouri, "Modeling the emergence of COVID-19: a systems approach," in 2020 IEEE 15th International Conference of System of Systems Engineering (SoSE), Jun. 2020, pp. 000445–000450. doi: 10.1109/SoSE50414.2020.9130555.

[13] B. Wang, O. Asan, and M. Mansouri, "Patients' Perceptions of Integrating AI into Healthcare: Systems Thinking Approach," in 2022 IEEE International Symposium on Systems Engineering (ISSE), Oct. 2022, pp. 1–6. doi: 10.1109/ISSE54508.2022.10005383.

[14] J. Ladyman, J. Lambert, and K. Wiesner, "What is a complex system?," Euro Jnl Phil Sci, vol. 3, no. 1, pp. 33–67, Jan. 2013, doi: 10.1007/s13194-012-0056-8.

[15] D. Wernli et al., "Building a multisystemic understanding of societal resilience to the COVID-19 pandemic," BMJ Global Health, vol. 6, no. 7, p. e006794, Jul. 2021, doi: 10.1136/bmjgh-2021-006794.

[16] D. Flanigan and K. Robinson, "Employing a Model Based Conceptual Design Approach to Design for Resilience," INCOSE International Symposium, vol. 31, no. 1, pp. 537–550, 2021, doi: 10.1002/j.2334-5837.2021.00853.x.

[17] B. Parsons, "Using Complexity Science Concepts When Designing System Interventions and Evaluations," 2010.

[18] M. Ruth and S. Goessling-Reisemann, "Chapter 1: Introduction to resilience of socio-technical systems," Cheltenham, UK: Edward Elgar Publishing, pp. 2-8, 2019. doi: 10.4337/9781786439376.00006.

[19] J. Amadi-Echendu and G. A. Thopil, "Resilience Is Paramount for Managing Socio-Technological Systems During and Post-Covid-19," IEEE Engineering Management Review, vol. 48, no. 3, pp. 118–128, 2020, doi: 10.1109/EMR.2020.3013712.

[20] T. Parsons, The Social System, 2nd ed. London: Routledge, 1991. doi: 10.4324/9780203992951.

[21] D. Ivanov and A. Dolgui, "A digital supply chain twin for managing the disruption risks and resilience in the era of Industry 4.0," Production Planning & Control, vol. 32, no. 9, pp. 775–788, Jul. 2021, doi: 10.1080/09537287.2020.1768450.

[22] T. Ţiclău, C. Hinţea, and B. Andrianu, "Adaptive and Turbulent Governance. Ways of Governing that Foster Resilience. The Case of the COVID-19 Pandemic," Transylvanian Review of Administrative Sciences, vol. 16, no. SI, pp. 167–182, Dec. 2020, doi: 10.24193/tras.SI2020.10.

[23] A. Sharifi, A. R. Khavarian-Garmsir, and R. K. R. Kummitha, "Contributions of Smart City Solutions and Technologies to Resilience against the COVID-19 Pandemic: A Literature Review," Sustainability, vol. 13, no. 14, p. 8018, Jul. 2021, doi: 10.3390/su13148018.

[24] M. Maor and M. Howlett, "Explaining variations in state COVID-19 responses: psychological, institutional, and strategic factors in governance and public policy-making," Policy Design and Practice, vol. 3, no. 3, pp. 228–241, Jul. 2020, doi: 10.1080/25741292.2020.1824379.

[25] M. Bruneau et al., "A Framework to Quantitatively Assess and Enhance the Seismic Resilience of Communities," Earthquake Spectra, vol. 19, no. 4, pp. 733–752, Nov. 2003, doi: 10.1193/1.1623497.

Solar Panel Efficiency in Oman

Ahmed Al-Aamri[1], Ali Al-Humairi[2&3], Ayham Al-Rahawi[1],
[1]Department of Engineering, [2]Department of Computer Secince, German University of Technology in Oman, Oman.
Emails: 15-0357@student.gutech.edu.om, ali.alhumairi@gutech.edu.om, ayham.alrahawi@gutech.edu.om

Hayat El Asri
Coventry University Wroclaw
Email: hayat.elasri@coventry.ac.uk

Peter Jung[3]
[3]Communication Technology, Duisburg Essen University, Germany
Email: peter.jung@kommunikationstechnik.org

***Abstract*—Solar panels are widely used in different locations and for different purposes including electricity production, satellites, mobile devices, and lights. It is also considered to be one of the cleanest and most renewable applications to produce electricity, yet there are various environmental factors that affect solar panel efficiency and production rate depending on the installed location. This paper aims to analyze the impact of dust accumulation on photovoltaic (PV) panel efficiency in Oman. The experiment is done on two different poles of solar cells, one oriented in the east direction and the other one on the west direction. The east side panels are cleaned daily; however, the west side panels are kept dirty to check the temperature and irradiance effect on solar panels efficiency and power output. The results show that the east solar panels were producing more efficiently than the west side due to the dust accumulation on the west side panels. The dust accumulation on the west side panels worked as a shading layer for the irradiance to enter the solar cells. However, the dust accumulation did not have any impact on temperature values, which was almost constant for both side panels.**

Keywords*—*Solar panel, Ambient temperature, Irradiance, Efficiency, Dust, Performance ratio.

I. INTRODUCTION

Scientists are always looking for sources of energy which have less pollution, are renewable, and thermodynamically free. In 1839, scientist Edmond Becquerel found that sunlight can cause electricity to come from metals and a few other scientists studied the relation between material, light and electricity, such as Albert Einstein. Then, a scientist called Russell Ohl made the first functional solar cell in 1954, which is similar to the ones used these days, and it is made from Silicon. Silicon (Si) material can be found in rocks or sand. Furthermore, this solar cell was enough to generate electricity for regular electrical devices. The solar cell became very useful in human life as it has been used widely in electricity production. As a result, in 1958, scientists used the solar cell in space satellite for the first time and it was used as the first power generation plant that can produce 1000 kW in 1982 in California, USA [1].

In 2014, Professor Shanaz Ghazi found that the North Africa and the Middle East (MENA) region are considered to have the highest dust collection area. In hot dusty areas, solar panels produce low electrical power due to the appearance of dust and the negative effect of dust on solar panel performance which can be daily, monthly, annually, or seasonally, in terms of time. Dust accumulation on PV modules tends to pose a reflection problem for the sunlight to enter the PV cells. As a result, solar panels absorb less irradiance and sunlight. This tends to generate less electrical power, which means low solar panel efficiency. Moreover, dust particle size varies with site and environment [2].

This paper is structured as follows. Section II presents the review of the literature and discusses the factors affecting solar panel performance and the dust factors and its adhesion on solar panels surface. Section III discusses the research objectives. Section IV discusses the case study and the experimental setup. Finally, Section V discusses the results.

II. LITERATURE REVIEW

This section discusses past works in factors that affect solar panel performance, soiling influence on photovoltaic panels (case studies) and dust properties on solar panels. This literature review is divided into 3 subsections to ensure extensive understanding of the subject matter.

A. Factors affecting solar panel performance

A solar panel does not exceed 20% of its efficiency worldwide, and there are several parameters that lead the solar panels to perform less than ideal [3]. In this subsection, the factors will be summarized in environmental terms.

High temperatures have a negative effect on solar panels. When the ambient temperature recorded is high, the power output and the efficiency of solar cells will decrease because of the high rate of the internal carrier recombination inspired by higher carrier concentration. The higher rate of internal carrier recombination occurs when the high temperature enters the solar cell. As a result of this phenomenon, the electrons inside the solar cell will recombine with positive charges instead of flowing in the negative charges path. This recombination generates electric charges collision which, in turn, results in thermal emissions (heat) inside the solar cell. Basically, solar irradiation and temperature are directly proportional to the photovoltaic cell temperature. Whenever the temperature of the solar cell increases, the current rises gradually, but the voltage will fall significantly, which translates into a big drop in power output and vice versa for low temperatures [4].

Another factor is the variation of solar irradiation. The differences of intensity of the solar irradiation which falls on the solar module influence some of the photovoltaic panel characteristics including open circuit voltage, power, short-circuit current, efficiency, and fill factor. The relation linking module voltage and module current is that, as the solar irradiance increases, the module currents increase too. Also, the relationship between module voltage and module power is that the power output will increase when the current increase due to their directly proportional relation. As a result, when the solar irradiance increases, the power output will rise as well [4].

The last main factor is soiling. Soiling can be in the form of accumulation of pollutants, bird fallings, dust, and dirt. In essence, soiling works as shading; it is a slim screen which enforces in solar panels and decreases the falling of sunlight on the cell. Dust is a solid particle with diameter less than 500 micro-meters. Soiling can happen when moisture condensates the dust particles which adhere to solar panel layers, especially at the lowest part of the tilted panel due to the gravitational force on the dust particles. The accumulation of soiling will make one thin layer, which can cause partial shading in the lower row cells. Moreover, the power output of photovoltaic system may decrease by 5% to 17% [4] due to the soiling factor. In terms of location, deserted areas and places near highways have more dust in compression to rainy areas. Also, it is better to put the solar panels on a roof top instead of ground solar panels to prevent dust and soil accumulation on the panels. The fine dust creates more performance loss than the large one; this is because the small particles have smaller gaps between each other so the light cannot pass through them [4].

B. *Dust and its adhesion on solar panels surface*

Soiling is known as a phenomenon that is affected by metrological factors and weather conditions. Furthermore, the parameters that influence the dust on solar panels can be divided into two groups: solar panel installation factors and environmental factors [5].

For the installation factors, horizontal surfaces tend to accumulate more dust than inclined surfaces. Additionally, small particles of dust settle on the tilted surface of solar panels, but the large particles of dust tend to roll down. This is due to the effect of the gravitational force on dust particles. Also, whenever the inclination angle of the solar panel increases, the gravitational force impact in dust accumulation increases. Environmentally speaking, dust has different properties which affect the precipitation on the solar panel surface. In terms of physical properties, the large size dust particles tend to drop off from solar panel screen and for the small size dust particles, they tend to stick to the solar panels surface [5].

C. *Critical dust analysis*

There are many studies regarding soiling influence on PV cells performance. Some of these experiments are discussed in this subsection.

The first study was in Saudi Arabia, Jizan region, specifically as part of the science collage of Jazan University. The researchers used two PV panels with two different angles (30° and 55°) which produce peak power around 30 watt per solar cells and were placed on the roof of a building. The median humidity in the Jazan region is around 70 percent, the temperature range is between 22 °C to 38 °C and speed of wind approximately 15 kilometer per hour, all throughout the year [6]. Readings were conducted every Monday at 11:30 AM for 112 days. At the beginning, the cells were washed with water to remove tiny particles to allow for detailed reading. The process of washing was performed whenever the panels got dusty [6]. Both tilted panels produced almost the same path (trend) of efficiency. What is more, the PV panels with higher tilt (55 degree) had a low amount of efficiency reduction compared to the solar panels with lower tilt (30 degree) because of the gravity force that eliminates a certain amount of dust particles spontaneously. Consequently, the total decrease of photovoltaic cells performance because of soiling collection in the Jazan area was approximately 9.7 percent for the 55 degrees panels and 10.4 percent for cells inclined at 30 degrees [6].

Another experiment was conducted in Iran, specifically at Tehran University in 1999. Numerous solar systems with various inclination angles have been mounted on the roof of the Tehran University building. The aim of this experiment was to examine the impact of air contamination from local industry and vehicles on the photovoltaic system performance seasonally [2]. The results showed that the system production differs with the season and that the level of contamination that occurs in the air in various seasons is the justification. The highest air pollution was in the winter season because the air has a high density. As a result, the irradiance is affected by contaminated air, and this leads to a reduction in solar cell performance. Since the climate is windy in the fall season, the dust or pollution frequently flies away, and the efficiency is better in the fall season. The highest performance is in the spring season due to the rainy weather that helps to remove the pollution or dust from the panels. Finally, the summer has an efficiency production amount between spring and fall. The tilt angle increases the production amount for all four seasons. Additionally, the efficiency values of solar panels decrease by more than sixty percent due to the phenomena of air pollution which settles on the surface of photovoltaic panels and works as shading [2].

III. RESEARCH OBJECTIVES

This experimental paper helps increase the performance ratio of the solar panel in Oman by checking the effect of dust and irradiance on the top surface of solar cell. Also, we investigated the number of cleanings needed per month for dusty solar panels.

The aim of this research work is to explore the influence of voltage and current parameters on the power output and the efficiency of solar cells and to check the impact of the environmental factor efficiency. The voltage and current are affected by two environmental factors, namely irradiance and temperature change.

IV. CASE STUDY AND EXPERIMENTAL SETUP

A. *Case study of solar panels*

In this subsection, the case study of the solar panel system is divided into sub-case studies. This includes the location of the solar panel system, the website used for the information of PV panel system and the devices or components utilized in the photovoltaic panel framework. Also, we present the experimental setup and the tools used for this study.

1) System

The system used in this study is Virtual Control Operator Room developed by meteo-control GmbH Company (mc). This system provides solar panels system data with graph analysis and location of solar panels system. It helps the technicians and clients to check the system to see if there are any problems. Also, it can be used to perform studies and research [7].

2) Location of the site

The research specifically takes place at the German University of Technology in Oman (GUtech), which is located in Halban, Muscat, Sultanate of Oman. The facility is located at a height of 41 meters (m) above sea level. The solar technology facility is structured by Shams Global Solution and British Petroleum Oman (BP Oman) [8].

3) System Components

The solar panels systems at GUtech consist of different components. Each component will be explained fully in this subsection.

The experiment is set up on a flat-roof zone, which is made from multi-crystalline cells 0.15675 × 0.15675 (m) and it is installed on a platform with a height of around 1.5 meters (m). The flat-roof solar module is subjected to two poles (east and west), and it has 12 panels (3 sets × 2 panels at the east × 2 panels at the west) and each panel consists of 72 (12x6) cells, as shown in Figure 1. The dimensions of one panel are: 0.992 m height, 1.960 m width, and 0.04 m depth and it weighs 2.25 kg. Also, the panels are placed at an angle of around 10° to get more sunlight. The panels are made by Trina-solar and the ID number is TSM-325-PD14 [9].

Figure 1. Flat-roof solar module at GUtech.

A Fronius inverter is used for the flat-roof system and its module number is Fronius Symo 3.0-3-M. The inverter dimensions are 0.645 m height, 0.431 m width and 0.204 m depth, and its weight is around 19.9 kg (with mounting plate). It produces at a maximum efficiency of 98% [10].

On site, there are two sensors used for all four zones, namely the weather sensor and the pyrano-meters. The flat-roof system has one more sensor that measures the panel temperature and irradiance which is called the Silicon irradiance sensor.

- Weather station sensor

To control the solar power plant's production and performance, a weather forecasting device can be incredibly useful, as shown in Figure 2. Additionally, it can be used for scheduling maintenance and washing periods. Fundamentally, it measures parameters like irradiance, other ecological factors like humidity, velocity of wind, direction of wind and module temperature [11].

Figure 2. Weather station sensor at GUtech

- Thermopile pyrano-meters

The thermopile pyrano-meter is an instrument used to detect the sun irradiance (intensity) from the hemispheric view of a flat surface incident. The sensor is made of a pyrano-meter structure, one or two domes, black body absorber and thermopile (it is an instrument which transforms the thermal energy absorbed from the sun in the form of electrical energy), as shown in Figure 3 [12].

Figure 3. Pyrano-meter sensor at GUtech

- Silicon irradiance sensor

This sensor is a solar cell made from Silicon and it can be used to measure the radiation because the relation between short circuit current and radiation is directly proportional. Also, it can measure temperature by connecting the temperature sensor to the Silicon irradiance sensor, as shown in Figure 4 [13]. The sensor is connected near the solar panels directly with the same angle, so it measures the solar irradiance that falls to solar panel directly.

Figure 4. Silicon irradiance sensor at GUtech

B. *Experimental setup*

This study took 91 days starting from the 6th of May, 2020. For the first 28 days, both side panels were kept dirty, and this was taken as the baseline. However, for the rest of 61 days, the east side of solar module was cleaned, and the west side of solar module was kept dirty.

At the beginning, the Virtual Control Operator Room website was explained by an employee who works at HTC to teach the user how to use the website and perform studies. Then, self-study of the website helped the user to learn more about the website and get familiar with it; in case the user did not understand something, he/she could go back to process number one (ask the HTC employer for more explanation). Then, an excel sheet was created to make studies and graphs analysis. The east side of the solar panels will be cleaned with a brush, microfiber cloth and water by a GUtech employee, taking time consumption and amount of water used into consideration. Then, the user will check for any sensor or technical problems; in case of any problem, he/she should ask for help from HTC employees and repeat the process starting with repeating the cleaning of the east solar cells. However, in case everything is fine, data can be withdrawn safely and if there is any big change in data due to weather or other side effects, notes should be written down. The process of cleaning, checking for any side effects or technical issues and withdrawal of data will be repeated daily for two months. After two months of repeating the same procedure, the final process will take place by analyzing graphs, comparing data and discussing.

V. RESULTS AND DISCUSSION

A. *Result analysis*

The experimental part focuses on analyzing the outcome of the results obtained, based on utilizing a comparison between different graphs for both solar panel sides (east (cleaned) and west (dirty)). These graphs include Irradiance-DC current, Temperature-DC voltage, and the DC power of photovoltaic panels. The results were collected from the 6th of May to the 5th of August, 2020. The data was taken daily from sunrise (6:00) to sunset (19:00) because the sun is most present during this time frame which leads the solar panels to produce power output. For the first 28 days, both panels were not cleaned, and this was taken as baseline. However, for the first 18 days, the amount of irradiance and temperature falls to solar cells were not stable due to the change in weather.

1) *Irradiance and DC current (East)*

Figure 5 shows the irradiance and DC current on the y-axis and the days number on the x-axis for the cleaned panels. As it can be seen on the graph, the relation linking irradiance and DC current is directly proportional and, from day one to day eighteen, both parameters generate a gradual decreasing line due to soiling accumulation. However, for the remaining 73 days, the production of both parameters remained constant because the east panels were cleaned. Most of the days, the irradiance which fell on the east solar module fluctuated between 552 W/m^2 and 432 W/m^2, and the DC current that was generated by east solar module averaged between 6.31 A and 4.80 A. On the 24th of May (day 18), the absorbed irradiance on the west solar cells was low from times 14:00 to 17:00 because of weather change which resulted in a low generated DC current, around 4.43 A. On day 39 (14th of June), the irradiance falling to the east solar module was around 510 W/m^2, but the generated DC current was 4.50 A which is out of the daily average range. This drop was due to a technical error that happened to the solar module which shows there was a problem in converting the absorbed irradiance to DC current and a gradual decrease in falling irradiance to solar module, specifically at 11:00.

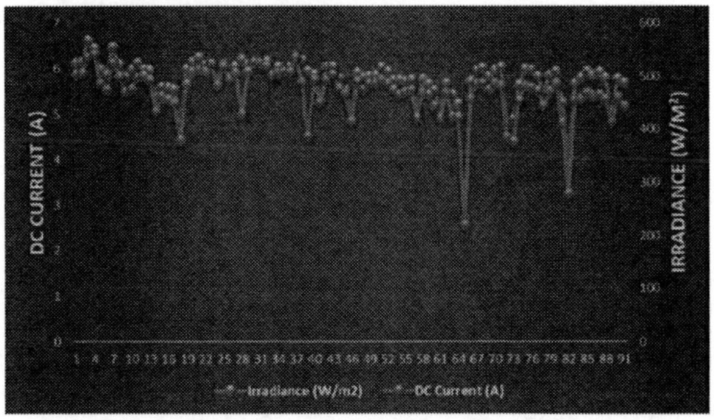

Figure 5. Experimental data of east panels between irradiance and DC current

Also, on day 72 and day 73 (17th and 18th of July), respectively, the absorbed irradiance by the east solar module was approximately 410 W/m^2 and 419 W/m^2 respectively, due to a reduction in temperature specifically from 12:00 to 14:00. As a result of DC current, the east solar panels generated 4.48 A and 4.40 A, respectively. The east solar module generated around 3.24 A on day 82 (27th of July) due to a technical error that happened to solar panels specifically at 12:00, appearing that the DC current was 0 A and low daily average solar irradiance exactly from 12:00 to 19:00 around 331 W/m^2 which fall to the east solar module.

The largest drop in the east solar module current output was on day 65 (10th of July). The solar module produced around 2.58 A. This was because of a low amount of falling irradiance to the east solar module, approximately 237 W/m^2, which was influenced by the presence of clouds.

2) *Irradiance and DC current (West)*

Figure 6 shows DC current and irradiance on the y-axis and the days number on the x-axis for the non-cleaned panels. As per the figure, the relation between irradiance and DC current is directly proportional and there is a steady decrease in the DC current from the first day to the last day. Additionally, the absorbed irradiance of the west solar module is constant and nearly the same as the one on the east side. The absorbed irradiance by the west solar module fluctuated between 445 W/m^2 and 571 W/m^2, but the DC current which was generated by the west solar module declined from the peak amount of 4.52 A to about 2.96 A.

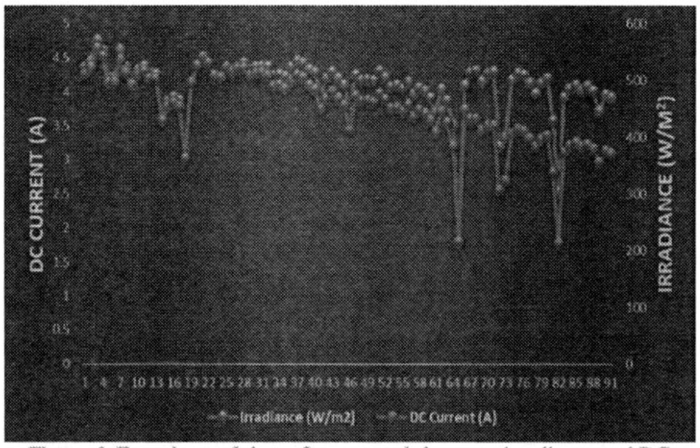

Figure 6. Experimental data of west panels between irradiance and DC current

On the 24th of May (day 18) the falling irradiance on the west solar cells was low in the afternoon from 14:00 to 17:00 due to weather change. As a result, the produced amount of DC current was 3.02 A. On day 72 and day 73 (17th and 18th of July) respectively, the absorbed irradiance by the solar module was around 383 W/m^2 and 399 W/m^2 respectively, due to a reduction in temperature specifically from 12:00 to 14:00. Accordingly, the west solar panels generated around 2.55 A and 2.67 A, respectively. A technical issue happened on day 82 (27th of July) to the west solar module exactly at 12:00, and the DC current produced was 0 A. This affected the daily produced DC current which reached around 1.79 A. Also, the daily solar irradiance to the west solar panels was around 304 W/m^2, which played a role in decreasing the current, especially from 12:00 to 19:00.

The highest decline in producing current by the west solar module was on day 65 (10th of July). The west solar module produced around 1.79 A. The problem on day 65 was a low amount of falling irradiance to the west solar module around 232 W/m^2 which was influenced by dust accumulation and the presence of clouds. Additionally, the effect of dust on the west solar modules started from day 67 (12th of July). Consequently, a high irradiance rate was absorbed by the silicon irradiance sensor, but vice versa for the solar panels, which shows low DC current rates.

3) Temperature and DC voltage (East)

Figure 7 shows cell temperature and DC voltage on the y-axis and the days number on the x-axis for the cleaned panels. It appears from the graph that the relation between cell temperature and DC voltage is inversely proportional and almost constant values for cell temperature and DC voltage for three months. The temperature at the east solar module was oscillating between 57.59 °C and 46.76 °C, and DC voltage which was produced by east solar module was between 178 V and 192 V, on average.

On the 21st of May (day 15), the east panels were having a technical error to convert the absorbed temperature to DC voltage due to dust accumulation on the Silicon irradiance sensor. Consequently, the relation between these two parameters is shown to be a directly proportional one. On day 57 and day 59 respectively, the cell temperatures of the east solar module were around 50.53°C and 46.53°C independently however, the generated DC voltages were 190.87 V and 183.23 V independently. Consequently, in these two days, the east solar module was having a technical error issue of measuring the absorbed temperature because the surrounding temperature was investigated to have an inverse proportion relation with cell temperature. Due to this issue, the relation between the cell temperature and the DC voltage was directly proportional. The cell temperature was 50.09°C on day 89 but the DC voltage was high (185.38 V) which shows the relation is direct proportional between these two parameters. As a result, from 9:00 to 10:00, the surrounding temperature was low around 33°C and this influenced the average DC voltage to increase.

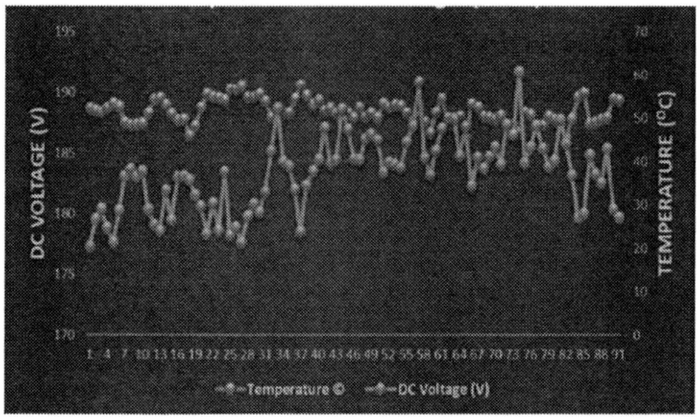

Figure 7. Experimental data of east panels between temperature and DC voltage

4) Temperature and DC voltage (West)

Figure 8 illustrates cell temperature and DC voltage on the y-axis and the days number on the x-axis for the non-cleaned panels. Evidently, from the chart, the relation between cell temperature and DC voltage is inversely proportional and there are almost constant values for cell temperature and DC voltage for three months. On most days, the temperature of the west solar module fluctuated between 57.76 °C and 47.88 °C, and DC voltage produced by the west solar module averaged between 182 V and 191 V.

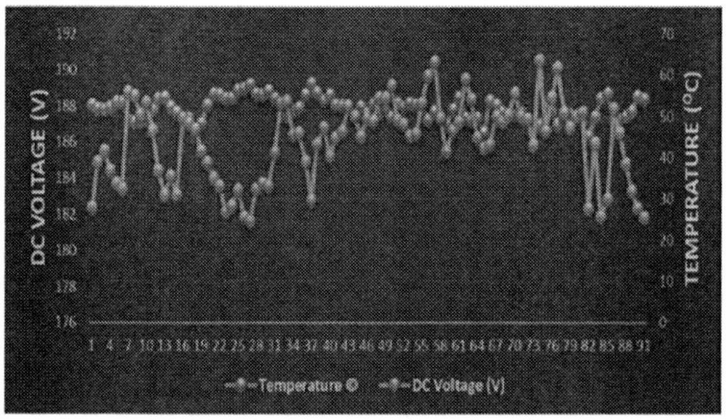

Figure 8. Experimental data of west panels between temperature and DC voltage

On day 15 (21st of May), the west module was having a technical error to transfer the absorbed temperature to DC voltage because of soiling on the Silicon irradiance sensor surface. As a result, the relation linking DC voltage and temperature is a directly proportional one. On day 82, day 85, and day 91 respectively, the cell temperatures of the west solar module were around 45.03 °C, 55.4 °C and 54.1 °C independently but, the generated DC voltages were 182.34 V, 182.82 V and 181.83 V independently. As a result, in these three days, the west solar module was having a technical error issue of measuring the absorbed temperature because the surrounding temperature was investigated to have an inverse proportion relation with the cell temperature. Because of this problem, the relation between the cell temperature and the DC voltage is shown to be directly proportional. In addition, during week five, exactly on day 57, day 59, day 61, day 63 and day 65 respectively, the cell temperatures of the west solar module were generating a direct proportional relation with the DC voltage. This was due to an error that happened to Silicon irradiance sensor which was affected by dust accumulation.

5) DC Power (East and West)

The DC power of the photovoltaic panels is influenced by the DC voltage and the DC current. Both factors have a direct relation to power output. Consequently, if there is any sudden drop, rise or change in the DC power data, then there would be a variation for either the DC voltage or the DC current.

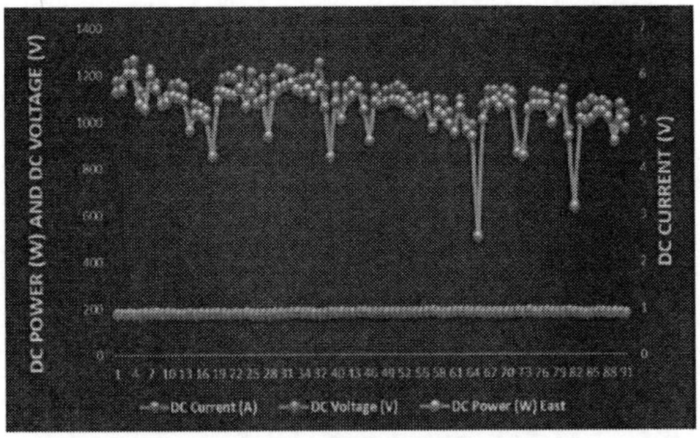

Figure 9. Experimental data of east panels between DC power, DC current and DC voltage

Figure 9 shows the chart between DC power, DC current and DC voltage on the y-axis and days number on the x-axis for the cleaned panels. Clearly, from the chart, the DC power is mainly affected by the DC current since the DC voltage produces a nearly constant line. The DC power which was generated by the east solar module was fluctuating between 1205 W and 917 W and it has a constant generating line.

Different days (18, 39, 72, 73 and 82) in Figure 5 show a sudden drop in the DC power which produces less than 860 W. This happened because of the low production in the DC current. The critical drop happened on day 65. It produced around 506 W. This was also due to a drop of the DC current to around 2.58 A.

Figure 10 depicts the DC power, the DC current and the DC voltage on the y-axis and the days number on the x-axis for the non-cleaned panels. From the chart, we see that the DC power is mainly affected by the DC current since the DC voltage is producing almost a constant line. Nonetheless, the DC power line is decreasing progressively from peak power around 907 W to minimum power approximately 569 W.

Several days (72, 73 and 82) in Figure 10 show dramatic decline in DC power generating less than 526 W, this happened due to low production in DC current. The maximum drop occurred on day 65, producing around 350 W. This was also attributed to a decrease in DC current to around 2.58 A.

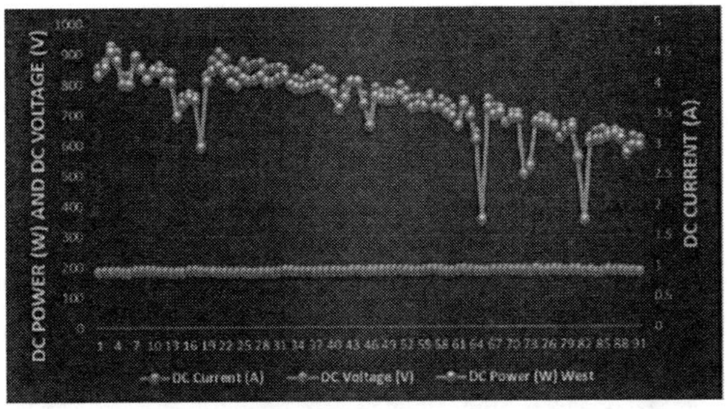

Figure 10. Experimental data of west panels between DC power, DC current and DC voltage

B. *Discussion on Results analysis*

From the above detailed analysis, it can be concluded that dust accumulation on solar cells affects the irradiance and current only because the cell temperature and voltage were constant for both panels. There were big differences between the amounts of DC power of the east panels compared to the west panels due to dust accumulation on the solar cell glass. The east panels generated more power than the west panels. Additionally, the power of the west panels started to drop in week six. As a result, the falling irradiance amount was almost the same for both panels, but the generated current of the west panels was low.

C. *Performance ratio (efficiency) analysis*

The performance ratio (PR) of the photovoltaic cell is calculated by taking the sum of the DC power produced by the PV cells at time (day) to the sum amount of irradiance multiplied by the sectional area of PV cells and efficiency. The PV cells efficiency varies with the irradiance rate and the DC power.

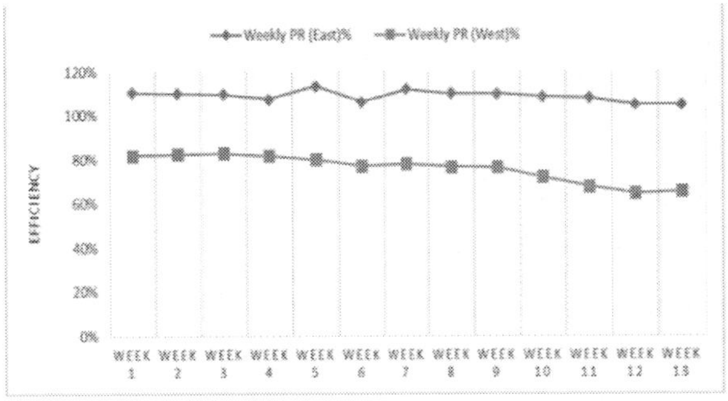

Figure 11. Solar panel efficiency

Figure 11 compares the performance ratio change during thirteen weeks for the east and the west panels. From the graph, the east panels tend to have a higher efficiency when compared to the west panels because they are cleaned daily for two months with no dust accumulation on their surface. The east panels generated constant values of efficiency between 113% maximum and 105% minimum for all thirteen weeks. The west panels started with a constant rate of efficiency between 83% and 81% for the first five weeks. After week five, the impact of dust on the west solar cells started to appear, the west panels generated a gradual decrease efficiency from 77% to 65%. As a result, the west panels' efficiency began to decrease weekly by approximately 2.2%.

D. Discussion on Performance ratio analysis

It can be concluded from the analysis of performance ratio that the east solar cells were more efficient than the west solar cells and produced constant values. This is because the east solar panels absorbed more irradiance compared to the west solar panels from sunrise to sunset in the summertime. Also, the dust accumulation tends to reduce the amount of irradiance on the west PV cells. The generated DC power for the east panels is higher than the west panels. Moreover, from the performance ratio analysis, it can be recognized that the performance ratio values of the east PV cells exceed 100% because of different reasons. One of these above-mentioned reasons is that the Silicon irradiance sensors for both sides were dusty, and this resulted in an error in reading the real integers. Additionally, the inclination accuracy of the Silicon irradiance sensor compared to the panels might affect the amount of absorbed irradiance which, in turn, affects the performance ratio. Another reason can be the relative humidity that could impact the Silicon irradiance sensor accuracy.

VI. CONCLUSION

The leading target of this experiment was to measure the dust effect on solar panel efficiency in Oman. A case study was performed to understand the working system of solar panels at the German University of technology in Oman and to plan for experimental setup. The experiment was done using two different poles of solar cells, one oriented in the east direction and the other one in the west direction. The east side panels were cleaned daily; however, the west side panels were kept dirty. This was done to compare the efficiency of the solar panels with and without dust accumulation.

The results show that the east solar panels were producing more current than the west side panels due to the dust accumulation on the west side panels which works as shading layer for the irradiance to enter the solar cells. The generated current from the east solar panels was almost constant between 6.31 A and 4.80 A, however, the west side of PV cells were producing a decreasing line, at maximum 4.52 A to about 2.96 A. In terms of voltage, both sides panels were producing almost the same amount of voltage, between 178 V to 192 V, with almost constant amount of absorbed temperature during the three months.

As a result of the analyses, the main factor that affects the power output and efficiency of the solar cells is the current which is environmentally affected by the irradiance amount. Moreover, the east solar panels were producing constant amount of power and efficiency, however, the west panels were generating a decreasing amount of power and efficiency. In addition, from the analysis of the irradiance-current, power and efficiency of dusty solar cells, we see that in week five, the influence of dust on solar cell performance generated low values for all three parameters.

REFERENCES

[1] R. Hantula, "How Do Solar Panels Work?" New York: Chelsea Clubhouse, 2010.

[2] M. R. Maghami, H. Hizam, C. Gomes, M. A. Radzi, M. I. Rezadad, and S. Hajighorbani, "Power loss due to soiling on solar panel: A review", Renewable and Sustainable Energy Reviews, pp. 1307-1316, 2016.

[3] D. R. Das, "Effect of Different Environmental Factors on Performance of Solar Panel", International Journal of Innovative Technology and Exploring Engineering (IJITEE), vol. 8, issue 11, pp. 15-18, 2019.

[4] D. Vidyanandan, "An Overview of Factors Affecting the Performance of Solar PV Systems", Energy Scan, vol. 27, no. 28, pp. 216, 2017.

[5] A. Shaju and R. Chacko, "Soiling of photovoltaic modules-Review", IOP Conf. Series: Materials Science and Engineering 396, pp. 1-10, 2018.

[6] R. Karmouch and H. E. Hor, "Solar Cells Performance Reduction under the Effect of Dust in Jazan Region", Journal of Fundamentals of Renewable Energy and Applications, pp. 1-4, 2017.

[7] Cockpit SGS' Training Centre, Retrieved June 18, 2020, from Hussam Technology Company: https://www1.meteocontrol.de/vcom/cockpit/index/systemId/1052369

[8] Shams Global Solutions and Partners, Retrieved June 19, 2020, from Shams Global Solutions: http://shamsoman.com/who-we-are/

[9] TSM-PD14, 2017, Retrieved June 21, 2020, from TALLMAX MODULE: https://static.trinasolar.com/sites/default/files/EN_TSM_PD14_datasheet_B_2017_web.pdf

[10] Fronius Symo, June 2020, Retrieved July 8, 2020, from Fronius: https://www.fronius.com/en/photovoltaics/products/all-products/inverters/fronius-symo/fronius-symo-3-0-3-m

[11] Why Do Solar Power Plants Need Weather Monitoring Station (WMS)? Retrieved June 28, 2020, from Aeron: https://aeronsystems.com/why-do-solar-power-plants-need-weather-monitoring-station-wms/

[12] Hukseflux, What is a pyranometer? Hukseflux Thermal Sensors, pp. 1-5, 2006.

[13] Ammonit, Silicon Irradiance Sensor MT. Retrieved June 22, 2020, from http://www.windup.pt/resources/pyranometer_siliconirradiancesensor.pdf